Bittern egg

Snipe egg

Banded
damselfly

Great ramshorn shell

Eyewitness
POND & RIVER

In association with
THE NATURAL HISTORY MUSEUM

Written by
STEVE PARKER

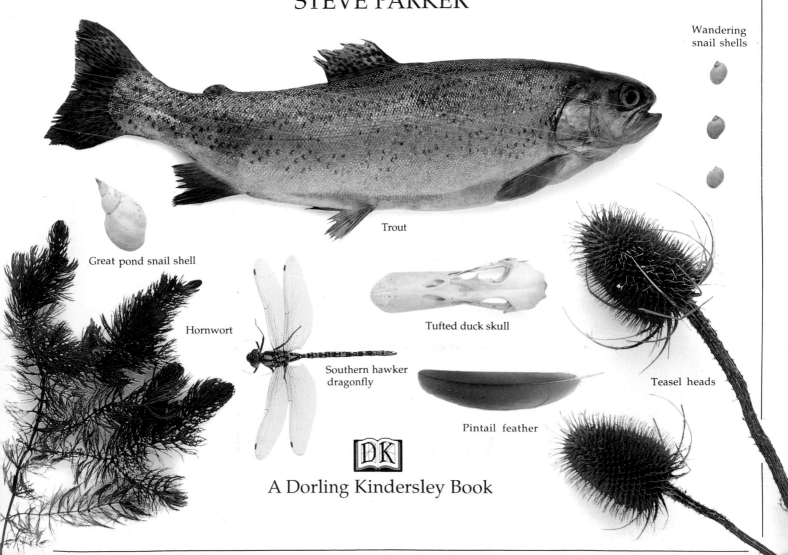

Wandering
snail shells

Great pond snail shell

Trout

Hornwort

Southern hawker
dragonfly

Tufted duck skull

Pintail feather

Teasel heads

DK

A Dorling Kindersley Book

Curly waterweed

Floating pondweed leaves

River snail

Yellow flag seeds

Fern

Waterbird feather

Water beetle

Bog pondweed leaves

Azolla water fern

Water boatman

Dragonfly larva

Water starwort

Three-spined sticklebacks

Waterbird feather

Marestail

Great pond snails

Water-lily leaves

Hornwort

DK

LONDON, NEW YORK, MUNICH,
MELBOURNE, and DELHI

Project editor Sophie Mitchell
Art editor Pamela Harrington
Managing art editor Jane Owen
Special photography Philip Dowell
Editorial consultants
The staff of the Natural History Museum London

PAPERBACK EDITION
Managing editor Andrew Macintyre
Managing art editor Jane Thomas
Senior editor Kitty Blount
Senior art editor Martin Wilson
Editor Karen O'Brien
Art Editor Ann Cannings
Production Jenny Jacoby
Picture research Lorna Ainger
DTP designer Siu Yin Ho

This Eyewitness ® Guide has been conceived by
Dorling Kindersley Limited and Editions Gallimard

Hardback edition first published in Great Britain in 1988.
This edition published in Great Britain in 2003
by Dorling Kindersley Limited,
80 Strand, London WC2R 0RL

Color reproduction by Colourscan, Singapore
Printed in China by Toppan Printing Co. (Shenzhen) Ltd.

See our complete
catalogue at
www.dk.com

Eyewitness
POND & RIVER

Swan mussel shell

Water snail shell

Common reed

Common reed
fruiting head

Otter skull

Kingfisher skull

Mayfly

Reedmace
fruit

Reed bunting nest
and eggs

Mallard egg

Great diving beetle

Kingfisher wing

Contents

Great ramshorn shell

Fool's watercress leaf

Hornwort leaf

Spring plants

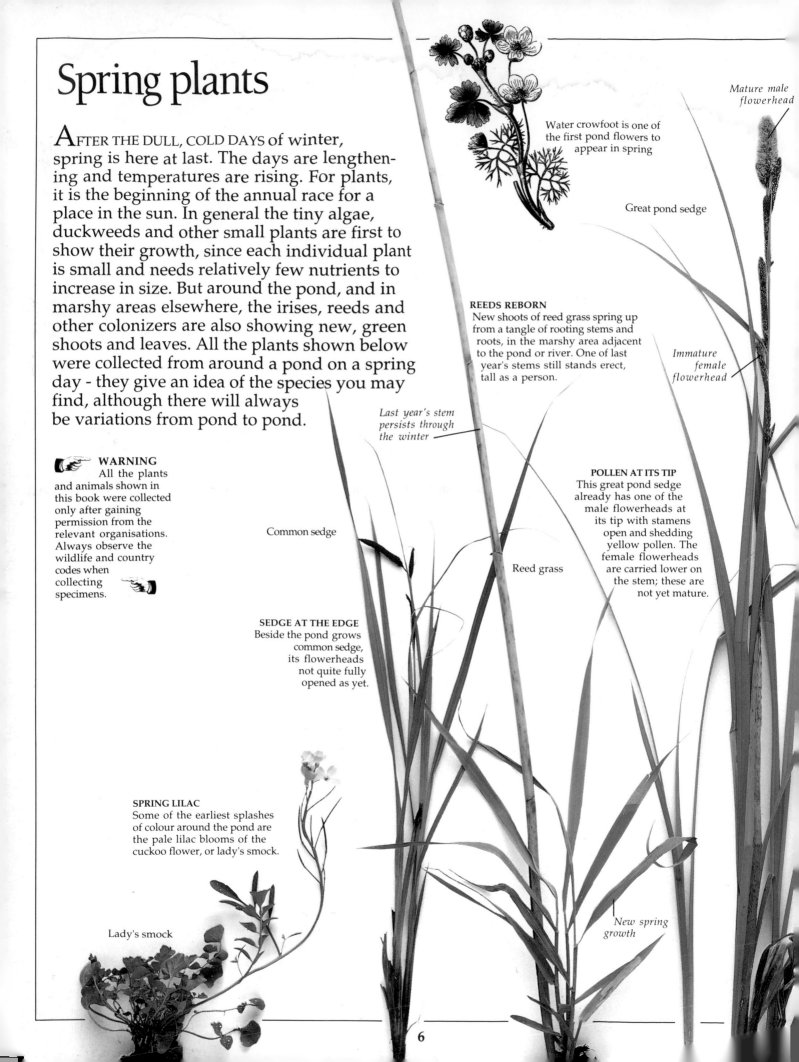

AFTER THE DULL, COLD DAYS of winter, spring is here at last. The days are lengthening and temperatures are rising. For plants, it is the beginning of the annual race for a place in the sun. In general the tiny algae, duckweeds and other small plants are first to show their growth, since each individual plant is small and needs relatively few nutrients to increase in size. But around the pond, and in marshy areas elsewhere, the irises, reeds and other colonizers are also showing new, green shoots and leaves. All the plants shown below were collected from around a pond on a spring day - they give an idea of the species you may find, although there will always be variations from pond to pond.

WARNING
All the plants and animals shown in this book were collected only after gaining permission from the relevant organisations. Always observe the wildlife and country codes when collecting specimens.

Water crowfoot is one of the first pond flowers to appear in spring

Mature male flowerhead

Great pond sedge

Immature female flowerhead

REEDS REBORN
New shoots of reed grass spring up from a tangle of rooting stems and roots, in the marshy area adjacent to the pond or river. One of last year's stems still stands erect, tall as a person.

Last year's stem persists through the winter

Common sedge

Reed grass

POLLEN AT ITS TIP
This great pond sedge already has one of the male flowerheads at its tip with stamens open and shedding yellow pollen. The female flowerheads are carried lower on the stem; these are not yet mature.

SEDGE AT THE EDGE
Beside the pond grows common sedge, its flowerheads not quite fully opened as yet.

SPRING LILAC
Some of the earliest splashes of colour around the pond are the pale lilac blooms of the cuckoo flower, or lady's smock.

New spring growth

Lady's smock

6

SEASON OF CATKINS
Willows, common trees of lake and river edges, greet spring with a fine display of furry catkins. These are the tree's flowers. Early bees and other insects visit the flowers for nectar and pollen, and act as pollinators. The wind also blows pollen from the golden male catkins to the greenish female ones, which are usually borne on a different tree.

Female catkins

Goat (pussy) willow

Weeping willow

Female catkins

FLAGS STILL FURLED
The yellow flag iris will soon be in bloom. Here, the new leaves grow up from the thick, spreading, underground stem. Their sword-like shape has given this plant the alternative name of sword flag.

Crack willow

Yellow flag

Sword-like leaves

THE PUSS MOTH
The caterpillar of this moth feeds on sallow, a kind of willow, and poplar leaves. Both these trees are common in damp or moist soils, so puss moths and their caterpillars are often seen near ponds and rivers.

Male catkins covered in yellow pollen

Last year's stem

KING OF THE FLOWERS
The brilliant yellow flowers of the marsh marigold, or kingcup, decorate pond edges and other damp areas almost as soon as the snows melt away. A snail or some other herbivore has already made a meal of one new leaf.

WATER PLANTAIN
A pale, woody stem is all that is left of last year's metre-high (3-ft) spray of flowers (p. 57). New leaves grow from a bulb-like base. Despite its name, the water plantain is not one of the true plantains, bane of the keen lawn gardener.

New spring growth

Marsh marigold

Leaf damaged by snail

Meadow rue

Delicate, notched leaves

Water plantain

SPRING FLUSH
A young meadow rue bears its first flush of distinctively notched leaves. It prefers damp' meadows and pond or stream banks.

Spring animals

As THE SPRING SUN'S WARMTH spreads through the water, animals begin to stir themselves from among the weeds and mud at the bottom of the pond. It is a time of urgent new life. Frogs and toads, fish and newts, are courting, mating and laying eggs. Their offspring soon hatch in the warming water, eager to cash in on the spring burst of life that provides food for all. "Cold-blooded" aquatic creatures become more active with the rising water temperature, and in a mild spring the smaller ponds, which warm up faster than large ones, are soon seething with newborn snails, insects, amphibians and many other creatures.

Frog spawn

Protective jelly surrounding egg

Black egg

THE SPAWN IS BORN
As early as January, adult frogs congregrate in ponds and prepare to mate and spawn (pp. 38-9). Around March the female lays up to 3,000 eggs, fertilized by the male, who clings to her back. The water-absorbing jelly around each egg swells, and soon the whole mass is many times her body size.

BIG BROTHERS AND SISTERS
Tadpoles hatch from spawn some two to three weeks after laying. The warmer the water, the faster they develop. Here, common frog tadpoles from a large, cool pond, only two weeks out of their eggs, mingle with four-weekers from a small pond that warmed up more quickly.

Tiny tadpoles from a cool pond

Tadpoles from a warm pond

This engraving of a water flea shows its complex anatomy

BORN ON TO THEIR FOOD
Each adult pond snail lays up to 400 eggs, embedded in a jelly-like "rope" attached to the underside of a submerged leaf on which the young snails will feed (p. 52).

Common toad

Dry, warty skin

A NEW LEAF
In spring water snails lay their eggs under leaves like these water-lily leaves.

Water-lily leaves

Protective jelly

Snail eggs

Pond snails

Water fleas

SPRING BLOOM
Water fleas and other minute animals and plants bring a pea-green soup look to many ponds in spring. This is the early "bloom" of micro-organisms that provide food for larger creatures.

TWO SEXES IN ONE
Many adult pond snails are hermaphrodites, having both male and female reproductive organs.

Damage to leaf edge caused by natural splitting

SECOND SPRING
This young water beetle, common in small ponds and ditches, may well be celebrating its second birthday. Two years ago it was an egg, in that autumn a larva, last spring a pupa, and last summer a newly emerged adult.

FIRST SPRING
A water beetle larva has large protrusible jaws ready to tackle and eat any small creature the spring pond has to offer. Some species stay as larvae for two years or more before pupating into adults (p. 51).

KING OF THE BEETLES
The great diving beetle is the king of the carnivores in many small ponds, feeding on tadpoles, small fish and almost anything else it can catch. In fact the dull, furrowed "back" (hard wing covers) on this one indicates it is not a king, but a queen - a female. The male's wing cases are smooth and shiny.

SOME WEEKS TO TAKE-OFF
A mayfly larva displays the characteristic three tails of this group. Despite its name, this larva might become adult and fly off in April or June (p. 50).

Female beetles have furrowed wing covers

Pale-green fronds

Water beetle

Water beetle larva

Erpobdella leech

Mayfly larva

Water slater

Crest along male's back

Male newt

Female newt

Duckweed

LOOKING FOR A WORM
The erpobdella leech loops through the water in search of a meal. This leech does not suck blood, but attacks worms and other soft-bodied small creatures and swallows them whole.

FINDING A MATE
The female water slater piggy-backs the male as he fertilizes the eggs, which she keeps in a pouch under her body.

BREEDING NEWTS
In spring the male newt develops a crest along his back and black spots over his skin. The female's skin remains olive-brown.

GREEN CEILING
In the spring sunshine, duckweed soon spreads across the pond (p. 44). The tiny fronds provide food for snails and insect larvae.

Common frog

Smooth, shiny skin

EARLY FLOWERS
The water crowfoot is an aquatic type of buttercup. The broad, flat leaves that float on the surface shade the water beneath, providing a good hiding place for fish.

Leaves that float on the surface are flat and broad

ONE-YEAR-OLDS
Apart from breeding adults, spawn and tadpoles, you may also find last year's babies around the pond in spring (pp. 38-9).

READY TO MATE
In spring, the male stickleback's throat and underside turn bright red (a red tinge can even be seen from above, as on the male shown here). In this breeding colouration, he entices the female to lay eggs in the nest he has built on the pond bed (p. 25).

Frogs lose their tail soon after emerging

Leaves that grow under water are finely divided

Male stickleback

Female stickleback

Early summer plants

THE RICHNESS AND VARIETY OF a pond's animal life are based on plants. Only a good growth of greenery, such as the plants shown here, all collected from a pond in early summer, will provide food, shelter and nesting sites for aquatic creatures. The kinds and abundance of plant life depend largely on how much sunlight the pond receives. Sunlight is the energy that ultimately powers life - and in summer it is in plentiful supply. Green plants capture the sun's light energy and transform it into chemical energy in their tissues - a process known as photosynthesis. When a herbivore eats a plant, it takes in some of this chemical energy; a carnivore does the same, obtaining from the herbivore what the herbivore took from the plant. Along the way, each plant and animal uses up some energy itself, transforming it into movement, new body tissues, seeds or eggs. A pond heavily shaded by trees will soon lose its vitality and richness of plants - and so of animals.

GROWING TALL
The straight stems of common reed are already shouldering their way above most other plants (p. 33). Most of the handsome flowerheads do not appear until late summer.

STRAPS OF LEAVES
The firm, strap-shaped leaves of reedmace stand as tall as a person. In a few weeks most of the familiar "brown poker" flowers will be visible (p. 33).

RAGGED PETALS
Ragged robin's pink petals have four long, straggly lobes. The plant thrives in many damp places, from pond banks to marshes.

Flowers appear for about two months in early summer

Ragged robin

Water arum

Tufted seeds

FLUFFY TUFTS
Cottongrass, an inhabitant of marshes and boggy pond sides, is a member of the sedge family (p. 32). When the ripe fruits develop they have unmistakable tufts of cottony hairs that catch the wind and disperse the seeds within.

UNPLEASANT SCENT
Common figwort frequents pond and stream banks, and also damp hedgerows and woods. The central flowerbud in each group is the first to open; the unpleasant scent attracts pollinating wasps.

Central flowerbud is first to open in early summer

Cottongrass

Common reed stem

Common figwort

RICHLY ROOTED
Water arum has thick, spreading stems with profuse roots.

Roots stabilize plant in shifting pond-edge soil

RIPENING FRUITS
Grey willow's leaves are more rounded than
the spear-shaped leaves of weeping willow.
This tree, also called the sallow, is developing
fluffy-covered fruits from the female
catkins (p. 7). Like most willows,
it roots well in damp ground
by ponds and rivers.

EMERGING FLOWERS
The yellow flowers of
the yellow flag iris are
just beginning
to unfurl from
their protective
sheaths (bracts).

Reedmace

Female catkin

Fluffy fruits

Bract

SEDGE SEEDS
In summer the fuzzy
yellowish flowerheads
of false fox sedge (p. 33)
darken to ripe seeds
ready for dispersal
along the
pond bank.

Grey willow

Style *Petal*

Sepal

*Darkening
seed heads*

**PETALS
AND SEPALS**
The "petals" of
the yellow flag
are, in fact, made
up of sepals, petals
and styles (the
female parts of the
flower that help to
receive the pollen).

Cone

False fox sedge

Yellow
flag

Marsh
horsetail

CONE-BEARER
The marsh horsetail
grows best in very
moist ground and
shallow water.
Horsetails do not bear
flowers, instead they
have cone-like structures
at their stem tips
(compare with the
marestail on p. 12).

Early summer animals

ᴇᴀʀʟʏ ꜱᴜᴍᴍᴇʀ is a time of thinning out and fattening up for pond animals. The swarms of young tadpoles, insect larvae and water snails feed greedily on the abundant plant growth of this season (pp. 10-11).

But they are gradually thinned out by larger predatory creatures, such as beetle larvae and dragonfly nymphs (p. 48), newts and small fish. These grow fat and in their turn may fall prey to larger carnivores, from frogs to fish, such as carp and tench, to visiting birds like herons, and perhaps to water shrew, mink and other mammals. And so the food chain of the pond builds up: plants first, then herbivores (plant-eaters), to carnivores (meat-eaters). But this is not the end. Death comes to all and, when it does, creatures such as water slaters move in to consume plant and animal remains. Droppings of all creatures enrich the water, providing minerals and other raw materials for fresh plant growth. So the nutrients go round and round, being recycled in the miniature ecosystem that is the pond.

Silver water beetle, wing cases lifted to show wings

Common toad

GOODBYE FOR THIS YEAR
A few of the dozens of breeding toads may still be hanging about near the pond. But most have now dispersed to their favourite damp corners, in hedges, under logs and among the undergrowth. They will not return to the pond until next spring.

Tadpoles with developing hindlimbs

PETAL-LESS FLOWERS
Marestail is a shallow-water plant of ponds and streams, around whose stems squirm and swim the numerous tiny pond creatures of this season. It bears tiny flowers without petals, where the leaves join the stem.

BACK LEGS FIRST
Frog tadpoles are now fewer in number; many of their siblings have fallen prey to fish, newts, diving beetles and dragonfly nymphs. They have their back legs, which appear after about seven weeks. This change in body shape, from tadpole to adult frog, is called "metamorphosis".

Great pond snail

GROWN UP
This great pond snail is nearing full size, at about 5 cm (2 in) long. It slides slowly over the bottom of the pond, eating decaying plant remains.

Marestail

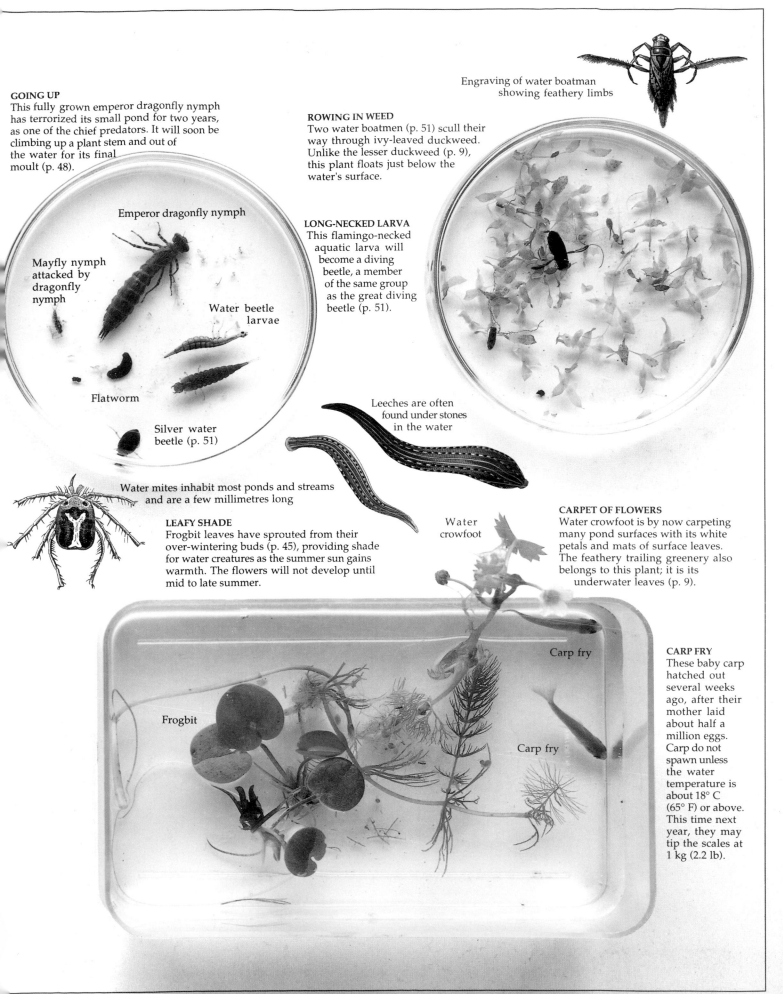

GOING UP
This fully grown emperor dragonfly nymph has terrorized its small pond for two years, as one of the chief predators. It will soon be climbing up a plant stem and out of the water for its final moult (p. 48).

Engraving of water boatman showing feathery limbs

ROWING IN WEED
Two water boatmen (p. 51) scull their way through ivy-leaved duckweed. Unlike the lesser duckweed (p. 9), this plant floats just below the water's surface.

Emperor dragonfly nymph

LONG-NECKED LARVA
This flamingo-necked aquatic larva will become a diving beetle, a member of the same group as the great diving beetle (p. 51).

Mayfly nymph attacked by dragonfly nymph

Water beetle larvae

Flatworm

Silver water beetle (p. 51)

Leeches are often found under stones in the water

Water mites inhabit most ponds and streams and are a few millimetres long

LEAFY SHADE
Frogbit leaves have sprouted from their over-wintering buds (p. 45), providing shade for water creatures as the summer sun gains warmth. The flowers will not develop until mid to late summer.

Water crowfoot

CARPET OF FLOWERS
Water crowfoot is by now carpeting many pond surfaces with its white petals and mats of surface leaves. The feathery trailing greenery also belongs to this plant; it is its underwater leaves (p. 9).

Frogbit

Carp fry

Carp fry

CARP FRY
These baby carp hatched out several weeks ago, after their mother laid about half a million eggs. Carp do not spawn unless the water temperature is about 18° C (65° F) or above. This time next year, they may tip the scales at 1 kg (2.2 lb).

Midsummer plants

THE MIDSUMMER POND is fringed with blooms of all hues, from the dusky pink of hemp agrimony to the many yellows of St John's-wort and the buttercups, and the tall purple loosestrife and rosy-red great willow-herb. Out on the water, lilies of various colours and the bright pink blooms of water bistort enhance the scene. Early-flowering species are by now fading, as their petals fall and their fruits form from the swelling lower part of the flowerhead.

Arrowhead

Flowering rush

Pink flowers on stalks

Developing fruits

RUSH IN BLOOM
The dark pink blooms of flowering rush are borne on stems up to 1.5 m (5 ft) tall. As explained on page 32 this is not a true rush, though its leaves are rush-like and grow in a rosette from the stem base. It is often planted to decorate ornamental ponds.

Common figwort

FROTHY FLOWER
Meadowsweet's tiny, creamy flowers combine to form a foamy mass carried on a firm stem, often more than 1 m (3 ft) tall. This relative of the rose likes pondsides, boggy areas and wet meadows.

Mass of tiny flowers

GROWN UP
The figwort shown on page 10 has now grown to its full height of almost 1 m (3 ft). The flowers are spaced at regular intervals on the upper section of stem.

FRUITS FORMING
The water arum's fruits are ripening as the specialized cup-shaped leaves, called spathes, around them begin to yellow and wither (see also p. 10).

Spathe

Developing fruits

Meadowsweet

Dark-green leaves have serrated edges

Water arum

Figwort's stem has a distinctive square cross-section

GREYISH-GREEN SHEEN
Osier, a typically water-loving willow, has extremely long, sharply pointed leaves. The tiny hairs on the underside of each leaf give it a greyish-green sheen.

Osier

Hawthorn

Haw

Water plantain's small pinky-white flowers bloom on tall, erect sprays of stems at this time of year (p. 57)

Dark green upperside of leaf

Grey underside of leaf

GREEN TO RED
Hawthorns tolerate wide variations in soil type and moisture content so this tree is often found growing by ponds. The green fruits are called "haws". In a few weeks the haws will turn a deep, rich red colour and attract birds such as waxwings and tits to the pondside.

WITHERED PETALS
The bright blooms (p. 10) of the yellow flag iris have withered to brown, and the fruit capsules are now forming. Each capsule resembles a chunky pea pod, and contains several knobbly seeds (p. 4).

Seed pods

ST JOHN'S-WORT
This plant (see also p. 16), grows in damp places such as shady woods and pond banks. The flowers begin to fade in midsummer.

SPHERES AND SPEARS
Its yellow flower indicates that greater spearwort is a type of buttercup. Two spherical, spiky heads of ripening fruits are shown, as well as the spear-shaped leaves that give the plant its name.

Withered flower

St John's-wort

Ripening fruit

Yellow flag

PINK FORGET-ME-NOT
Water forget-me-not flowers throughout the summer, in damp and shady places. Its stems trail along the pond edge, and its flowers may be blue, white or pink.

Spear-shaped leaves

Water forget-me-not

Greater spearwort

15

Midsummer animals

MIDSUMMER IS A TIME OF GROWTH and departure in the pond. The frantic spring and early summer rush of new life is quietening. The surviving youngsters of this year's eggs, now fewer in number, settle down to the serious business of growing, laying down food stores and preparing for shorter, colder days ahead. Frog and toad tadpoles have become transformed into air-breathing mini-adults, ready to leave the water and take their first hops on land. A few young newts may stay in gill-sporting tadpole form through the coming autumn and winter, but others, now adult in shape, are also moving away. The exodus from the pond continues as aquatic insect larvae of many kinds develop into adults (p. 50), from tiny gnats, midges and mosquitoes to the mighty dragonflies (p. 48) that prey on them.

Tiny gnats (male and female) dance above the pond's surface during long summer evenings

Not rowing but flying, this water boatman shows its strong wings (p. 51)

Water snail

Growth rings

RINGS AND BANDS
Periods of slow growth are visible on this watersnail's shell. They are the thin rings towards the opening, that cross the spiral banding pattern.

HAPPY WANDERER
The wandering snail is more tolerant of soft water (p. 52) than, for example, the great pond snail - and so is more widespread in ponds and slow rivers.

Toadlet

Newtlets

Gills

Toadlet

NEWTLETS
These young newts still retain their gills, to help absorb oxygen from the warm summer pond water. They hide among weeds, eating water fleas and other tiny creatures.

TOADLETS
Toad tadpoles by now have grown their front legs and lost their tails, to resemble their parents. In midsummer they leave the pond for life on land.

BABY BIVALVES
In about ten years, these young freshwater molluscs will grow many times this size (p. 52). In their early years they are busy feeding and absorbing calcium from the water to build their shell.

Young freshwater molluscs

Wandering snails

Snail emerging from shell

SQUARE STEM
There are several species of St John's-wort (p. 15). This is square-stemmed, which lines watersides, marshes and damp hedgerows.

Square-stemmed St John's-wort

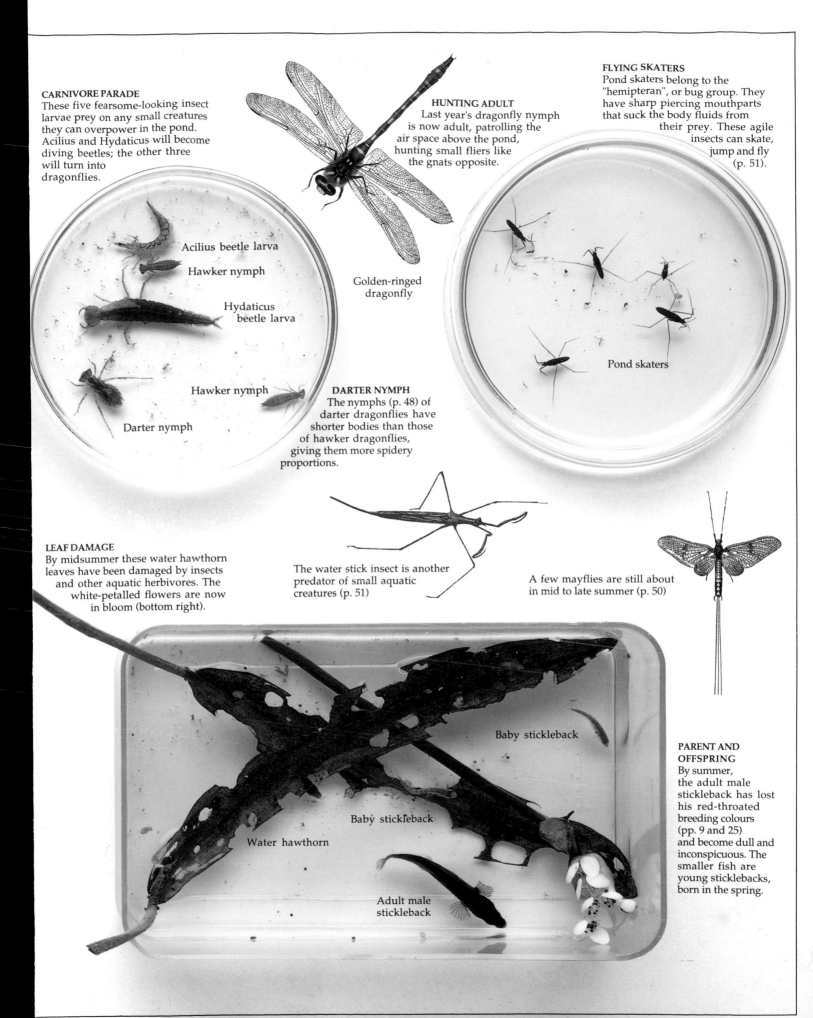

CARNIVORE PARADE

These five fearsome-looking insect larvae prey on any small creatures they can overpower in the pond. Acilius and Hydaticus will become diving beetles; the other three will turn into dragonflies.

Acilius beetle larva

Hawker nymph

Hydaticus beetle larva

Hawker nymph

Darter nymph

HUNTING ADULT

Last year's dragonfly nymph is now adult, patrolling the air space above the pond, hunting small fliers like the gnats opposite.

Golden-ringed dragonfly

FLYING SKATERS

Pond skaters belong to the "hemipteran", or bug group. They have sharp piercing mouthparts that suck the body fluids from their prey. These agile insects can skate, jump and fly (p. 51).

Pond skaters

DARTER NYMPH

The nymphs (p. 48) of darter dragonflies have shorter bodies than those of hawker dragonflies, giving them more spidery proportions.

LEAF DAMAGE

By midsummer these water hawthorn leaves have been damaged by insects and other aquatic herbivores. The white-petalled flowers are now in bloom (bottom right).

The water stick insect is another predator of small aquatic creatures (p. 51)

A few mayflies are still about in mid to late summer (p. 50)

Baby stickleback

Water hawthorn

Baby stickleback

Adult male stickleback

PARENT AND OFFSPRING

By summer, the adult male stickleback has lost his red-throated breeding colours (pp. 9 and 25) and become dull and inconspicuous. The smaller fish are young sticklebacks, born in the spring.

The pond in autumn

GRADUALLY THE SUN'S ARC across the sky flattens, and the hours of daylight shorten. Although the rays may still be warm in mid-afternoon, this is in marked contrast to the increasing chill of the night. Autumn has arrived, and pond wildlife is slowing down and preparing for winter. Summer-visiting birds have departed, but their place will soon be taken by waterfowl such as the Brent goose, Bewick swan and pintail duck (p. 28), that fly in from their far-north breeding grounds to enliven larger ponds, lakes and marshes. Mammals and resident birds feed greedily on the ripe fruits, building up their fat stores for the winter. However, their shelters and hiding places are gradually being whittled away, as the cold wind rattles crackly brown leaves from their stems, making the pond's banks look bare and untidy.

MASSED PARACHUTES
The dark spearhead-shaped seeds of hemp agrimony each bear a thick tuft of white hairs. These act as a parachute, aiding seed dispersal in the wind. This is a plant of marshy pondsides and wet fields.

Fluffy seeds ready for dispersal by autumn winds

STOUT PERENNIAL
Common figwort's small reddish-brown flowers (p. 14) have been pollinated by wasps, and the small greeny-brown, pear-shaped fruits are now developing. Figwort will be growing in the same place again next year, since this plant is a perennial.

Seed pods

Common figwort

Hemp agrimony

Developing seed pods

Hard rush

Seedhead on stem

Compact rush

Seedhead on stem

False fox sedge

Seedhead at end of stem

Flowering rush

Fruits

RUSHES AND SEDGE
The stiff stems of rushes and sedges bear autumn-brown seedheads. The stems usually persist into the winter, and are harvested for a variety of uses (p. 32).

FRUITING RUSH
Each of the flowering rush's blooms (p. 14) has developed into a six-sectioned fruit; inside each section there are many miniscule seeds. Like figwort, this plant is a perennial.

WINTER POKER
Reedmace's familiar brown "poker" of seeds stands guard over marshes and ponds, usually throughout the winter. In spring the poker bursts to scatter the fluffy-haired seeds.

Brown "poker" full of seeds

SNAILS SLOWING DOWN
Falling water temperatures mean that even pond snails begin to move about more slowly, tending to stay in deeper water.

Pond snails

Caddis fly cases

Alder cones

Alder

ALDER "CONES"
In autumn the alder's green fruits ripen to a browny-black colour and stay on the tree during winter. They are sometimes mistaken for small pine cones, but the alder is not a conifer. It prefers pond banks and streamsides, and its light seeds drop onto the water and float to new ground.

Reedmace

Newtlet

Dragonfly nymph

HOME IN A TUBE
Rectangular leaf fragments stuck into a spiral pattern and curled into a tube, signal the larval case of the great red sedge, a type of caddis fly (p. 50). These larvae will emerge as adult flies next year.

Seed pods

NEXT YEAR'S ADULT
Dragonfly nymphs found in the pond at this time of year will overwinter and emerge next year.

RECYCLING FUNGI
Animal and plant corpses are digested by fungi and their nutrients made available for recycling. Here, an old pondside tree was attacked and weakened by bracket fungi.

Yellow flag

AUTUMN JUVENILE
A young common newt, still equipped with gills, will overwinter as a "juvenile", and finish its transformation into an adult next year.

Bracket fungi grow on the outside of the trunk

ON THE BOTTOM
Leaves, twigs and other debris blow into the pond, or are washed in by heavy autumn rains. This accumulation of debris, overlying the mud of the pond bed, will shelter all manner of small water creatures during the winter months.

SOON TO SET SEED
The seed capsules of the yellow flag iris are now thick with ripening brown seeds (compare the same "pods" on p. 15). Eventually the fleshy capsule walls dry out and split into three boat-shaped segments; these peel back to release the seeds (p. 4).

Oak leaf

Willow leaf

Birch leaf

Willow twigs

The pond in winter

WHERE DO FLIES GO IN THE WINTER? More to the point, where do pond snails, flatworms, aquatic larvae, fish, amphibians and other pond creatures go in the winter? There are several strategies for surviving the season of cold and ice. "Cold-blooded" animals can generally live in the coldest water, provided they are not trapped in solid ice. Fish, and some water insects, molluscs and worms, move to the deepest part of the pond, to avoid being iced in. As the water cools, they do too, and their bodies need less and less energy, so they can survive with hardly any food. Cold water holds more dissolved oxygen than warm water; and supplies are enriched by various types of waterweeds, which can carry out photosynthesis (p. 46) using the frosty sunlight that penetrates the layer of ice. Coupled with the reduced needs of the inactive animals, this means there are sufficient supplies of oxygen for life, even when the pond is iced over for days. Another strategy, adopted by many very small water creatures, is to lay eggs in the autumn; the adults die and the eggs hatch next spring. Amphibians, such as frogs and toads, sleep through the winter in a sheltered place on land.

Water-lily leaf

Common reed

LAST REMAINS
Water-lily and arrowhead leaves still bear their long, anchoring stems - but the leaves are now browned, tattered and torn by waves, wind and frost.

POND SKATERS
Humans are active above, while animals and plants overwinter below.

WINDBURNED REED
Common reed flowerheads stubbornly resist winter's gales and snowstorms. Even the leaves stay stuck to the stems, though the combined effects of frost and windblasting turn them to crinkly brown ribbons.

Arrowhead leaf

Old leaves are evidence of the trees that grow round the pond

BLANKETS OF LEAVES
Decay is slow in the icy water. Shed leaves settle in blanket-like layers, which protect and insulate the small creatures and the winter buds of plants sandwiched between them.

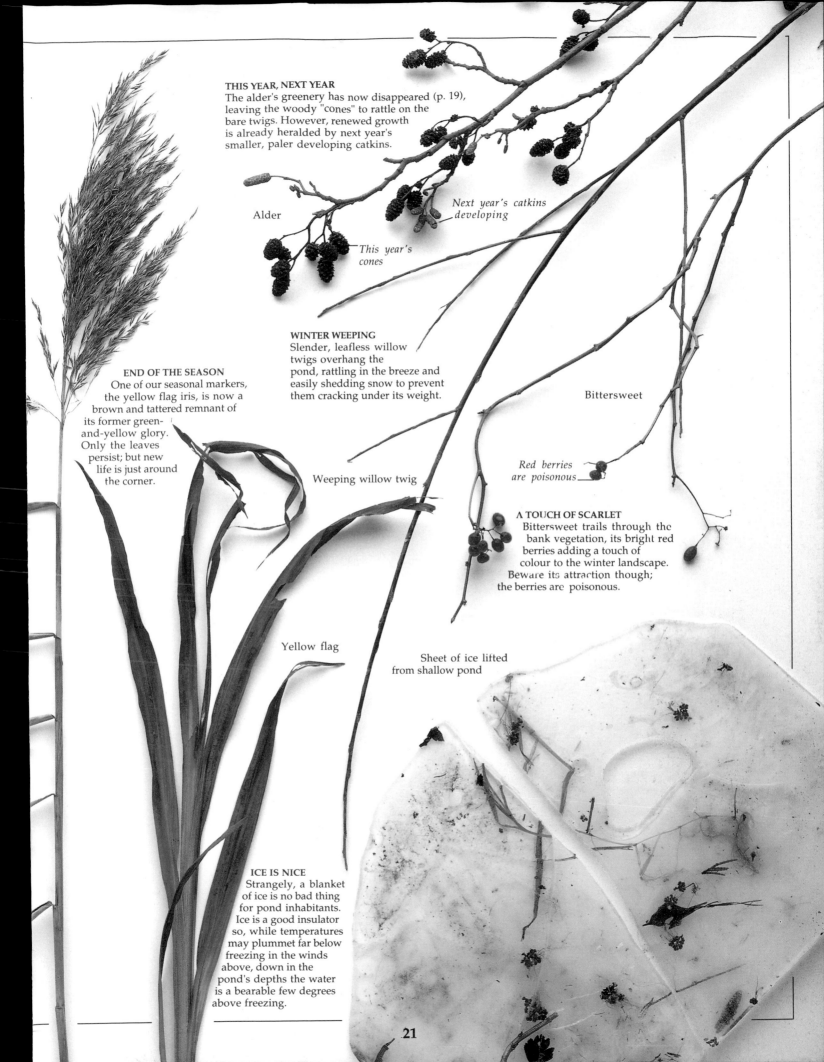

THIS YEAR, NEXT YEAR
The alder's greenery has now disappeared (p. 19), leaving the woody "cones" to rattle on the bare twigs. However, renewed growth is already heralded by next year's smaller, paler developing catkins.

Alder

Next year's catkins developing

This year's cones

WINTER WEEPING
Slender, leafless willow twigs overhang the pond, rattling in the breeze and easily shedding snow to prevent them cracking under its weight.

Bittersweet

Red berries are poisonous

Weeping willow twig

END OF THE SEASON
One of our seasonal markers, the yellow flag iris, is now a brown and tattered remnant of its former green-and-yellow glory. Only the leaves persist; but new life is just around the corner.

A TOUCH OF SCARLET
Bittersweet trails through the bank vegetation, its bright red berries adding a touch of colour to the winter landscape. Beware its attraction though; the berries are poisonous.

Yellow flag

Sheet of ice lifted from shallow pond

ICE IS NICE
Strangely, a blanket of ice is no bad thing for pond inhabitants. Ice is a good insulator so, while temperatures may plummet far below freezing in the winds above, down in the pond's depths the water is a bearable few degrees above freezing.

Freshwater fish

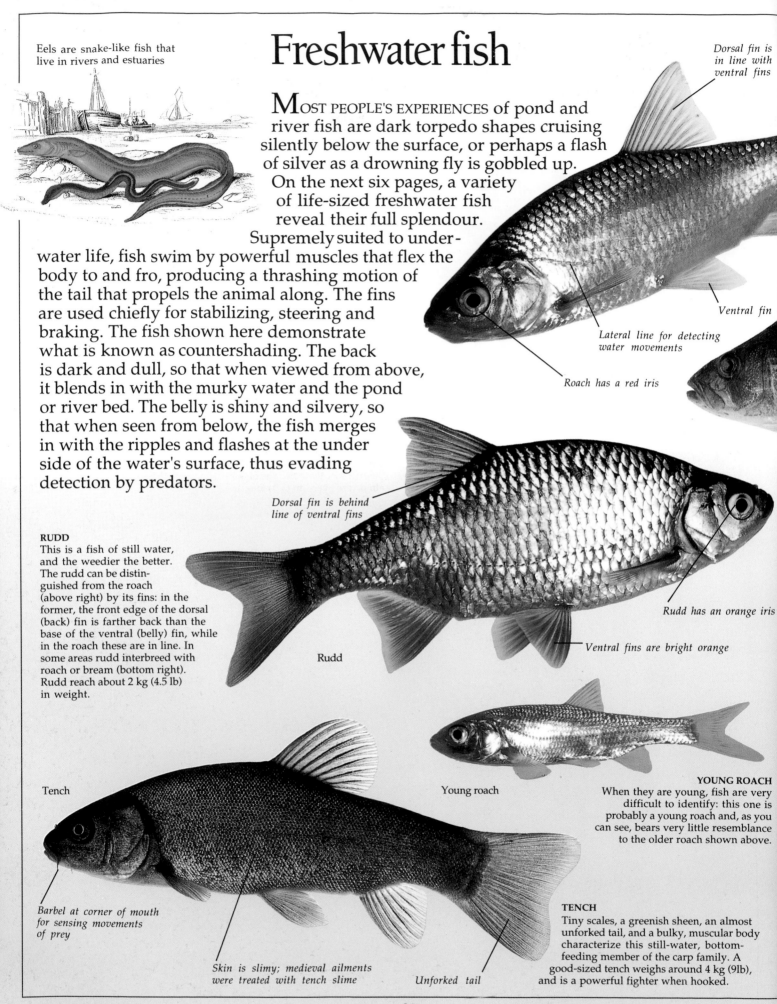

Eels are snake-like fish that live in rivers and estuaries

MOST PEOPLE'S EXPERIENCES of pond and river fish are dark torpedo shapes cruising silently below the surface, or perhaps a flash of silver as a drowning fly is gobbled up. On the next six pages, a variety of life-sized freshwater fish reveal their full splendour. Supremely suited to under-water life, fish swim by powerful muscles that flex the body to and fro, producing a thrashing motion of the tail that propels the animal along. The fins are used chiefly for stabilizing, steering and braking. The fish shown here demonstrate what is known as countershading. The back is dark and dull, so that when viewed from above, it blends in with the murky water and the pond or river bed. The belly is shiny and silvery, so that when seen from below, the fish merges in with the ripples and flashes at the under side of the water's surface, thus evading detection by predators.

Dorsal fin is in line with ventral fins

Ventral fin

Lateral line for detecting water movements

Roach has a red iris

Dorsal fin is behind line of ventral fins

Rudd has an orange iris

Ventral fins are bright orange

RUDD
This is a fish of still water, and the weedier the better. The rudd can be distin-guished from the roach (above right) by its fins: in the former, the front edge of the dorsal (back) fin is farther back than the base of the ventral (belly) fin, while in the roach these are in line. In some areas rudd interbreed with roach or bream (bottom right). Rudd reach about 2 kg (4.5 lb) in weight.

Rudd

Tench

Young roach

YOUNG ROACH
When they are young, fish are very difficult to identify: this one is probably a young roach and, as you can see, bears very little resemblance to the older roach shown above.

Barbel at corner of mouth for sensing movements of prey

Skin is slimy; medieval ailments were treated with tench slime

Unforked tail

TENCH
Tiny scales, a greenish sheen, an almost unforked tail, and a bulky, muscular body characterize this still-water, bottom-feeding member of the carp family. A good-sized tench weighs around 4 kg (9lb), and is a powerful fighter when hooked.

ROACH

The roach is a common, widespread fish that tolerates waters from clear rivers to muddy, mildly polluted canals. It is an unfussy eater, taking both plant and animal food. Roach are superficially similar to rudd (below left) and dace. They live for about 10 years, and the largest grow to 2 kg (4.5 lb) in weight.

Roach

SALMON BYPASS

On its way upriver to spawn, a big salmon can leap 3 m (10ft) out of the water to clear waterfalls and other obstacles. But, however, weirs, locks and dams have increased the number of hazards. One answer is the man-made salmon "ladder", that the fish can negotiate in easy stages.

Markings on flanks camouflage perch among waterweeds

Dark spot on spiny dorsal fin

Perch

Engraving of an adult salmon shows how the tail is thrashed from side-to-side to provide power for leaping out of the water

SALMON

The "king of fish" hatches in gravelly, fast-flowing water. It spends the first three or so years of its life in a river, and is known as a "parr" (resembling the trout parr on p. 27). It then migrates to the sea, becoming more silvery and known as a "smolt". After one to four years feeding on small fish and crustaceans at sea, mature adults return to the river of their birth to spawn. Most then die. The biggest salmon are over 1 m (3 ft) long and weigh 25 kg (55 lb) or more.

PERCH

The five or so dark vertical bars on the flanks, the two dorsal fins - the front one with prominent spines - and the reddish ventral and anal fins, mark out the perch as an exceptionally handsome fish. This youngster of one to two years may weigh 2 kg (4.5 lb) when fully grown. Perch feed on worms, crustaceans, molluscs, insects and small fish.

Ventral fins are tinged orange

Lateral line

Dorsal fin

BREAM

Deep-bodied, large-scaled bream frequent still and slow-flowing waters. They feed on small water animals such as insect larvae, and some water plants. The largest bream attain a length of about 80 cm (2.5 ft) and weigh about 4.5 kg (10 lb). The "stripe" along a fish's side, showing especially clearly here, is the lateral line. It is a groove of specialized tissue that detects vibrations in the water, in effect allowing the fish to "hear" and "feel" water movements.

Deeply forked tail

Group of bream

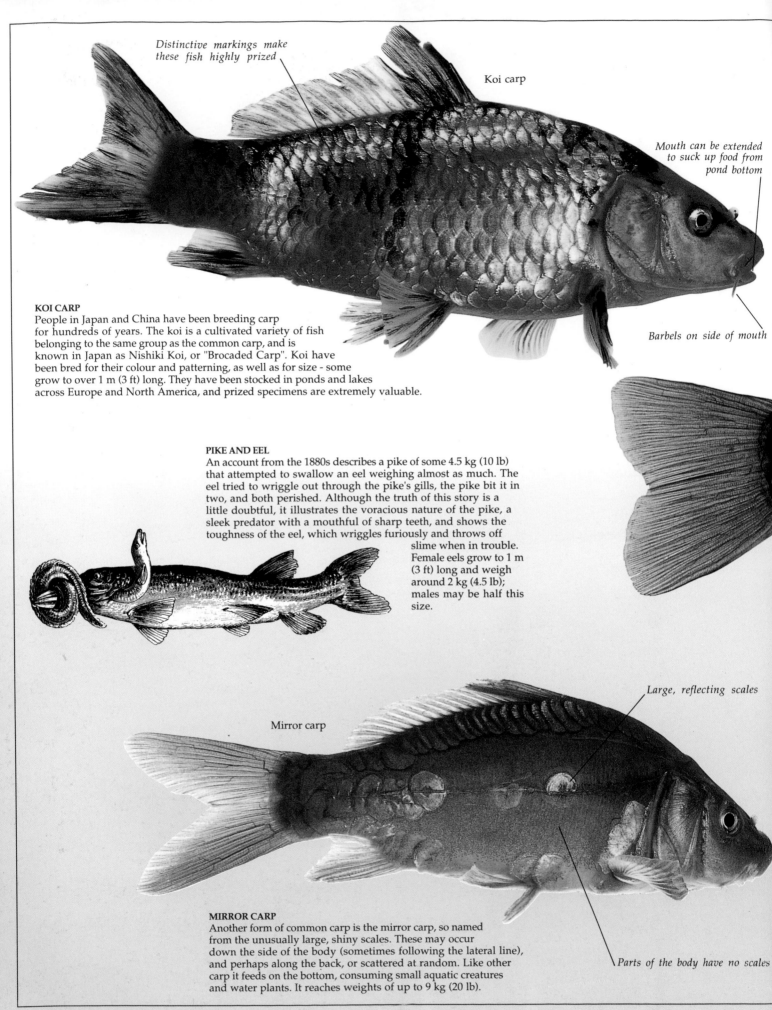

Distinctive markings make these fish highly prized

Koi carp

Mouth can be extended to suck up food from pond bottom

Barbels on side of mouth

KOI CARP
People in Japan and China have been breeding carp for hundreds of years. The koi is a cultivated variety of fish belonging to the same group as the common carp, and is known in Japan as Nishiki Koi, or "Brocaded Carp". Koi have been bred for their colour and patterning, as well as for size - some grow to over 1 m (3 ft) long. They have been stocked in ponds and lakes across Europe and North America, and prized specimens are extremely valuable.

PIKE AND EEL
An account from the 1880s describes a pike of some 4.5 kg (10 lb) that attempted to swallow an eel weighing almost as much. The eel tried to wriggle out through the pike's gills, the pike bit it in two, and both perished. Although the truth of this story is a little doubtful, it illustrates the voracious nature of the pike, a sleek predator with a mouthful of sharp teeth, and shows off the toughness of the eel, which wriggles furiously and throws off slime when in trouble. Female eels grow to 1 m (3 ft) long and weigh around 2 kg (4.5 lb); males may be half this size.

Large, reflecting scales

Mirror carp

MIRROR CARP
Another form of common carp is the mirror carp, so named from the unusually large, shiny scales. These may occur down the side of the body (sometimes following the lateral line), and perhaps along the back, or scattered at random. Like other carp it feeds on the bottom, consuming small aquatic creatures and water plants. It reaches weights of up to 9 kg (20 lb).

Parts of the body have no scales

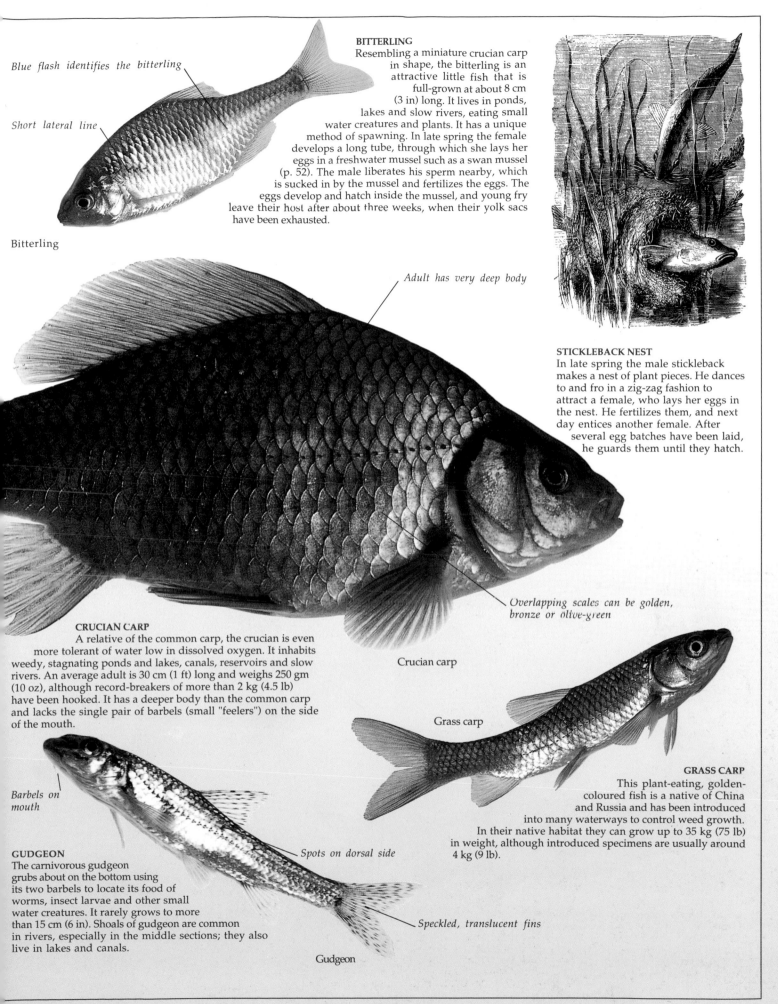

Blue flash identifies the bitterling

Short lateral line

Bitterling

BITTERLING
Resembling a miniature crucian carp in shape, the bitterling is an attractive little fish that is full-grown at about 8 cm (3 in) long. It lives in ponds, lakes and slow rivers, eating small water creatures and plants. It has a unique method of spawning. In late spring the female develops a long tube, through which she lays her eggs in a freshwater mussel such as a swan mussel (p. 52). The male liberates his sperm nearby, which is sucked in by the mussel and fertilizes the eggs. The eggs develop and hatch inside the mussel, and young fry leave their host after about three weeks, when their yolk sacs have been exhausted.

STICKLEBACK NEST
In late spring the male stickleback makes a nest of plant pieces. He dances to and fro in a zig-zag fashion to attract a female, who lays her eggs in the nest. He fertilizes them, and next day entices another female. After several egg batches have been laid, he guards them until they hatch.

Adult has very deep body

Overlapping scales can be golden, bronze or olive-green

Crucian carp

Grass carp

CRUCIAN CARP
A relative of the common carp, the crucian is even more tolerant of water low in dissolved oxygen. It inhabits weedy, stagnating ponds and lakes, canals, reservoirs and slow rivers. An average adult is 30 cm (1 ft) long and weighs 250 gm (10 oz), although record-breakers of more than 2 kg (4.5 lb) have been hooked. It has a deeper body than the common carp and lacks the single pair of barbels (small "feelers") on the side of the mouth.

GRASS CARP
This plant-eating, golden-coloured fish is a native of China and Russia and has been introduced into many waterways to control weed growth. In their native habitat they can grow up to 35 kg (75 lb) in weight, although introduced specimens are usually around 4 kg (9 lb).

Barbels on mouth

Spots on dorsal side

GUDGEON
The carnivorous gudgeon grubs about on the bottom using its two barbels to locate its food of worms, insect larvae and other small water creatures. It rarely grows to more than 15 cm (6 in). Shoals of gudgeon are common in rivers, especially in the middle sections; they also live in lakes and canals.

Speckled, translucent fins

Gudgeon

The trout

FEW FRESHWATER FISH match the trout for natural beauty and grace, for fighting power when hooked - and for taste when cooked! Trout belong to the salmon family. The brown trout and sea trout are, in fact, different forms of the same species. The former lives all its life in fresh water; the latter feeds in the sea and enters its home stream in summer, to breed in autumn. Adult brown trout may approach 1 m (3 ft) in length, while sea trout can be half as long again. There are many intermediates between these two forms, and distinguishing between them is difficult, as sea trout darken when they have been in fresh water for a few weeks and resemble the brown trout. In any case, trout vary enormously in appearance, depending on where they live, the nature of the water, the type of stream or lake bed, and the food they eat. Rainbow trout are another trout species altogether.

TYPICAL TROUT COUNTRY
An ideal trout stream - clear and cool running water, high in dissolved oxygen, with a gravelly bed for spawning. Trout are also found in clean lakes, usually in the shallows near their food.

Lateral line

Movements of the very mobile pectoral fins enable the fish to swim upwards or downwards

STREAMLINED PREDATOR
Brown trout, like other trout, are carnivorous. Food varies from tiny water fleas, flies, aquatic insect larvae (such as caddis larvae) and freshwater shrimps, to shellfish and other molluscs. The big "ferox" brown trout, from large, deep lakes, prey on other fish such as char or whitefish.

Brown trout

COLOURS OF THE RAINBOW
Rainbow trout were originally found in western North America (especially California). Like the brown trout, there are sea, lake and river forms. Their eggs were brought to Europe in the 1910s, and these fish have since been introduced into many rivers, reservoirs and lakes, to provide sport for anglers and food. Rainbow trout breed in some large reservoirs, but rivers have to be regularly stocked with young produced on "trout farms". The rainbow trout can live in warmer, less oxygenated water than the brown trout, so they are stocked in small lakes and large ponds where the brown trout would probably not survive.

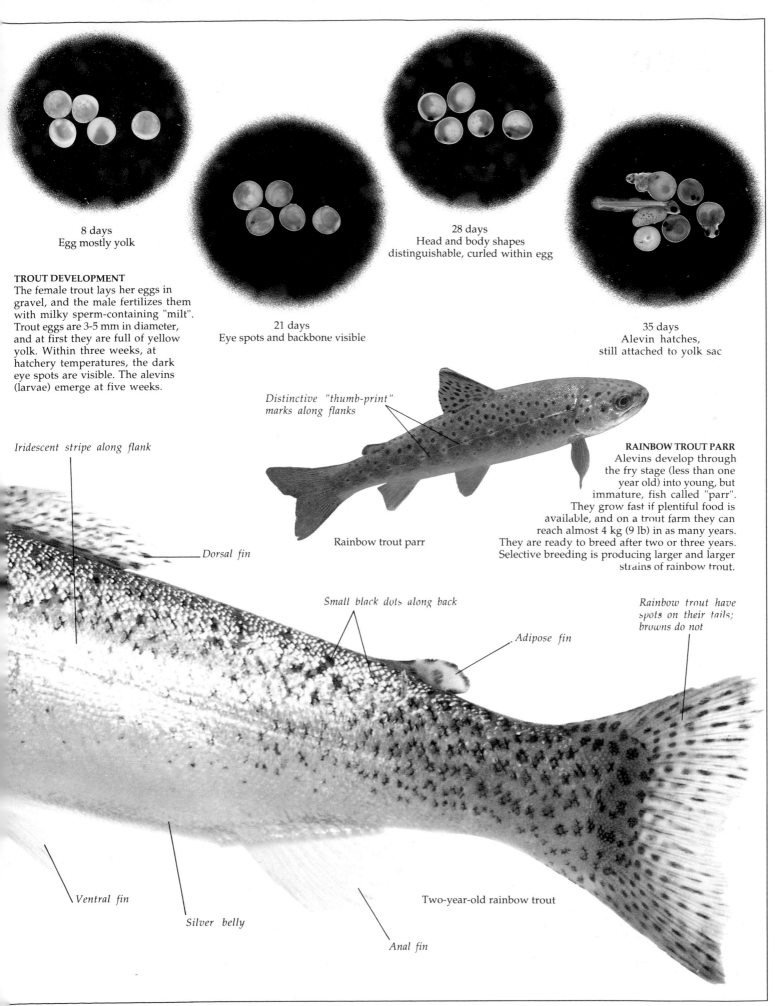

8 days
Egg mostly yolk

21 days
Eye spots and backbone visible

28 days
Head and body shapes
distinguishable, curled within egg

35 days
Alevin hatches,
still attached to yolk sac

TROUT DEVELOPMENT
The female trout lays her eggs in gravel, and the male fertilizes them with milky sperm-containing "milt". Trout eggs are 3-5 mm in diameter, and at first they are full of yellow yolk. Within three weeks, at hatchery temperatures, the dark eye spots are visible. The alevins (larvae) emerge at five weeks.

Distinctive "thumb-print" marks along flanks

RAINBOW TROUT PARR
Alevins develop through the fry stage (less than one year old) into young, but immature, fish called "parr". They grow fast if plentiful food is available, and on a trout farm they can reach almost 4 kg (9 lb) in as many years. They are ready to breed after two or three years. Selective breeding is producing larger and larger strains of rainbow trout.

Rainbow trout parr

Iridescent stripe along flank

Dorsal fin

Small black dots along back

Adipose fin

Rainbow trout have spots on their tails; browns do not

Ventral fin

Silver belly

Anal fin

Two-year-old rainbow trout

Waterfowl

Water and its resident wildlife attracts an amazing variety of birds. Quite at home on ponds, lakes and rivers (as well as seashores) across the world are about 150 species of wildfowl, including swans, geese and ducks. These generally heavy-bodied birds have webbed feet for swimming, and long, mobile necks for dabbling in the water and rummaging in the muddy bed for food. During spring, the dense bank vegetation provides many species with safe and sheltered nesting sites. In summer, the proud parents can be seen leading their fluffy chicks across the water. Aquatic plants and animals are a ready source of food for most of the year. In winter, when ponds freeze over, many wildfowl retreat to parks and gardens where they feast on scraps donated by well-wishing humans. Others fly south, often covering vast distances to find a more favourable climate in which to spend the winter.

Eider duck nest and eggs

Soft down feathers insulate the eggs in the nest

Teal nest and eggs

SPECIALLY GROWN DOWN
Ultra-soft eiderdown feathers grow on the female eider duck's breast. She plucks them to cocoon her eggs as she nests on sea or lake shore or river bank.

TEAL NEST
The teal makes its nest in dense undergrowth. The female is very careful when visiting her chicks, so as not to attract predators.

TUFTED DUCK EGG
The six to 14 eggs are laid in a nest close to the water's edge. The chick hatches after 25 days in the egg, and within a day it is swimming.

Teal, one of the smallest ducks

Nest would be lined with down when being used

ON THE WING
All wildfowl are strong fliers, many covering vast distances during their annual migration.

Vane

Quill

Flight feathers

FROM THE MOULT
Water-dwelling birds depend on their feathers to keep them dry, and much time is spent preening to keep the feathers in good condition.

ECLIPSE
Out of the breeding season, the pintail drake moults to his inconspicuous "eclipse" plumage, which resembles the female's colouring.

Pintail wing

MALE AND FEMALE
In the breeding season, most male ducks, like the pintail (far right), have bright plumage to catch the female's eye. The female (right) is duller, for camouflage on the nest.

Tufted duck

PARTIAL TO MUSSELS
The tufted duck feeds on freshwater mussels, as well as small fish, frogs and insects.

Tufted duck skull

MUSCOVY DUCK
This native of Central and South American ponds and marshes has a broad bill that takes aquatic plants and animals alike.

Muscovy duck

Muscovy duck skull

BEWARE THE ORANGE BILL
The mute swan's bill is normally covered by an orange sheath. Male swans can be extremely vicious, particularly in the breeding season when defending their territory.

Swan

The broad bill shape is suitable for dabbling for water vegetation

Mute swan skull

Waterbirds

Kingfisher wing

A STRETCH OF WATER acts as a magnet for all types of bird life. Many species, from sparrows to pheasants, come to drink. Others come to feed, from the tall, elegant heron that stands motionless as it watches for prey, to the flash of shimmering blue that signifies a kingfisher diving for its dinner. Bank plants, floating and submerged waterweeds, fish, frogs, insect larvae, shellfish and other aquatic life provide food for many birds. Some species, like reed buntings and warblers, find security in the impenetrable reed beds and dense waterside vegetation. Here they nest and raise their chicks, safe from predators such as foxes and hawks.

Kingfisher

THE EXPERT ANGLER
The brilliantly coloured kingfisher dives from its favourite perch for fish, tadpoles and shellfish. The broadsword-shaped bill is ideal for stabbing or spearing fish, then holding the slippery prey until it can be beaten into stillness on a branch and swallowed headfirst.

The white eggs have a glossy surface

Kingfisher eggs

KINGFISHER WING AND TAIL
The electric colours act as a warning to predatory birds, advertizing that the flesh is foul-tasting.

Tail and wing markings vary from species to species

Short wings beat rapidly when flying

Sharp bill for stabbing fish

Kingfisher tail

Kingfisher skull

WHITE EGGS
Kingfishers nest in a streambank burrow up to 1 m (3 ft) long, hence the white eggs - no need for camouflaging colours.

Long, sharp bill for spearing fish

Heron skull

Heron

LONG AND LANKY
Herons inhabit ponds, marshes and rivers, stalking fish and frogs in the shallows.

HERON'S HARPOON
The heron's fearsome bill makes an excellent fish-stabbing spear. This bird stands patiently until prey comes within reach, then darts out its long neck, stabs the victim, tosses it round and swallows it whole.

Bittern skull

BITTERN
This bird points its bill skywards and sways with the reeds to avoid detection. It can also climb up reed stems. The bittern builds a shallow platform of reed leaves and stalks, hidden deep in the reed beds. The five to six eggs take four weeks to hatch.

STEALTHY STALKER
The bittern is a solitary, daytime feeder, using its pointed bill to catch frogs, small fish and insects.

Reed warbler
nest

Reed warbler

*Nest is made from
reed flowerheads and
other vegetation*

*Nest is woven
round reed stalks*

SNIPE EGG
The colouring
camouflages the eggs
in the nest of this
small wading bird.

LITTLE GREBE EGG
White when laid,
eggs get discoloured
by plants and mud.
The little grebe is
also known as the
"dabchick".

WATER RAIL EGG
Water rails are shy
birds of waterside
undergrowth. There
can be as many as
15 eggs in a clutch.

HERON EGG
The blue eggs are laid
in well-defended nests
built of sticks and
twigs.

Reed bunting

FINE RUSHWORK
The reed bunting's nest is
built by the female alone,
although both parents feed
the chicks on insects and
their larvae.

DEEP CUP
The reed warbler's nest
is supported by several
stems, usually of
common reed. Its cup is
extra-deep, so that the
eggs and chicks do not
fall out when high
winds blow the reeds
over at an angle.

*The nest is made of
grasses and moss*

Reed bunting nest

Rushes and reeds

ALTHOUGH THEY LOOK quite similar, rushes and reeds are botanically very different. Sedges are often confused with rushes and reeds too. A rush is a grass-like plant with a round, usually solid stem and narrow, rigid leaves. A reed is a type of grass, usually tall, with feathery flowerheads and the strap-like leaves typical of the grass family. A sedge is a grassy-looking plant but not a true grass; its stem is usually solid and triangular in section unlike a grass's round, hollow stem. Despite their differences, these plants all have one thing in common - a liking for the wetness of marshes, pond edges and riverbanks.

Developing fruits

Hard rush

TINY FRUITS
The dark flowerheads of the lesser pond sedge bear the tiny fruits called utricles.

Loose cluster of tiny flowers

HARD RUSH
Rushes are related to the lilies, but their smaller, wind-pollinated flowers could not be more different.

Common reed stalk and leaves

NOT A RUSH
Despite its name and appearance, the flowering rush is not a true rush. Its name probably comes from its tall, rush-like stem and leaves, and the fact that it grows in the same habitat as true rushes.

Flowering rush

Lesser pond sedge

Stalk remains standing in winter as a hard cane

Rose-pink flowers grow on leafless stalks

REED WEED
The common reed grows almost too well in virtually any damp place, from brackish reaches near the coast to marshy areas and the banks of ponds, lakes and slow-flowing rivers. It stands up to 3 m (9 ft) tall, and is considered a weed in some water-ways (p. 34).

Rush-like leaves

Male flowers release clouds of pollen

Female flowers are fertilized by wind-carried pollen from male flowers and fluffy seeds are released when the flowerhead splits open

Great reedmace

Ten to 20 male flowerheads

Branched bur-reed

Two to four female flowerheads

Male and female flowers in the same flowerhead

False fox sedge

BRANCHING OUT
Each stem of branched bur-reed bears both male and female flowers. The smaller, ball-shaped ones towards the tip are male; the female ones are larger and spiky, rather like a rolled-up hedgehog.

Triangular stem has sharp edges if rubbed downwards

FALSE FOX SEDGE
On top of sharp-edged stems sit the tufty, yellow-green flowerheads containing both male and female flowers.

Branched bur-reed

TWO HEADS IN ONE
The great reedmace's poker-shaped flowerhead is in two parts. Above are hundreds of golden pollen-bearing male organs, and below are thousands of tiny female flowers packed into the brown cigar-shape. The whole resembles the mace, a weapon of medieval knights, hence the name. The plant is commonly, but wrongly, called the bulrush, after the painting of *Moses in the Bulrushes* (p. 35).

Flower stalk

Bract at base of each branch of flower stalk

33

The reed bed

THE REED BED IS THE SILENT INVADER OF OPEN WATER. Dense growths of tall, marshy-ground plants, such as reedmace and common reed, spread around the pond's edge by thick underground stems (rhizomes). These grow sideways through the mud towards the water and send up fresh shoots at intervals. They spread into the shallows, pushing aside water-lilies and marestails. The strong new reed stems slow any water movements and trap current-borne particles. At the end of each season the old leaves, stems and fruits add to the accumulating tangle. Within a few years previously open water can be turned into thickly vegetated marsh. Some years later the reed bed has moved on, still swallowing up the shallows, and drier-ground plants such as osiers and sallows (types of willow) have moved in at the back of the bed. This conversion of water to land by characteristic stages is an example of "ecological succession".

WATER TO DRY LAND

Shown below are characteristic plants of pond and lake edge, with sallows and sedges higher up the shore, reed beds towards the middle, and marestails and long-stemmed lilies in deeper water. As the reeds spread and invade the water, this becomes clogged and marshy and, over the years, the whole pattern of plant growth moves towards the centre of the pond. Of course, this does not happen in all bodies of water. People clear or harvest the reeds, while feeding animals, storms, flood currents and plant diseases keep a natural balance.

Fool's watercress

A REED ROOF OVER THEIR HEADS

The strong, long-persisting reeds are used as roofing material in many regions, from huts in Egypt and Sudan, to houses on stilts in Indonesia, and wooden cabins in southern North America. The English thatch style (above) offers excellent rain-repelling and insulating features.

A skilled thatcher working with quality reeds can make a roof that remains weatherproof for 40 years or more.

CREEPING CRESS

The fool's watercress gets its name because its leaves resemble true watercress. It is found in large quantities at the back of many reed beds, its horizontal, straggling stems adding to the general tangle of vegetation.

READY FOR RECYCLING

The thick, black mud of the reed-bed areas is rich in decaying plant and animal remains. Its nutrients are soon recycled by the rushes, reeds and other plants.

Reed-bed mud

Dry land

Marshy area

Shallow water

Open water

Underground rhizome

Horizontal stems

Sweet flag   Long straight
                    stalks

Flowerhead
may be 2.5 m
(8 ft) above
the roots

Dark-greeen
leaves have pale
undersides

EARLY HARVEST
The reed cutter's season is usually
the tail-end of winter and early spring.
Last year's stems are cut near the base,
before this year's shoots emerge,
so ensuring a future harvest.

THICK AND FLESHY
The juicy, strap-shaped leaves of sweet flag
sprout from a thick horizontal stem, itself
bearing many small roots which help in the
process of binding the glutinous marshy mud.

Osier shoot

The thin leaves
dry very quickly
when picked

Top of common
reed stem

MOSES IN THE . . . ?
As a baby, Moses was supposedly hidden in
a basket in a reed bed on the Nile's banks to
avoid detection. Illustrations showing this
are titled *Moses in the Bulrushes* although
most versions portray the baby in a clump
of reedmace. This confusion has led to the
name "bulrush" being popularly applied
to reedmace (p. 33); the true bulrush
resembling in general form
the spike rush.

WILLOWS FOR WEAVING
Osiers are found at the back of reed
beds, on less marshy ground. They
have long, straight shoots and a
shrubby shape. They are often
coppiced (cut at ground level)
to provide pliant stems ("withies")
for woven chairs and baskets.

THE STRAIGHT AND NARROW
The straight, narrow stems of common
reed are ideal thatching material.
They are also used to make paper and
other pulp-based materials. Plant growth
in reed beds is often relatively fast, with
plenty of water and nutrients, and slender
stems and leaves that allow light to
penetrate to the lower levels.

Base of common
reed stem

Waterside mammals

FRESHWATER HABITATS, from rivers and streams to the marshy edges of lakes and ponds, provide a home and food for a number of mammals. All the "aquatic" mammals shown here have fur coats adapted to their watery habitat. The fur of a mink, for example, is of two main types. Long, thick, flattened "guard hairs" provide physical protection and camouflaging colouration. For each guard hair there are 20 or more softer hairs of the underfur, only half as long, which trap air to keep water out and body heat in. The owners sensibly spend much time combing and cleaning their fur, keeping it in tip-top condition. Another adaptation for watery life is webs between the toes, for more efficient swimming.

FURRY FORAGER
The water shrew's dark-furred body is only about 9 cm (3 in) long. This bustling insectivore often lives in a bankside system of narrow tunnels that press water from its coat as it squeezes through. It eats small fish, water insects and even frogs, and forages on dry land for worms and other small creatures.

Mink

ADAPTABLE CARNIVORE
Minks are less specialized hunters than otters and, besides fish, will take birds, aquatic insects and land animals such as rabbits. The broad, webbed back feet provide the main swimming power.

American mink skull

Canine teeth

Molar teeth

TOOTHLESS "BEAK"
When a baby platypus hatches it has teeth, but these are soon lost. Adults grind up the food of shellfish, water insects and worms using horny plates along their jaws.

TEARERS AND SHEARERS
The mink's four long canine teeth, towards the front of its mouth, are built for catching prey and tearing flesh. The molars, at the back, are ridged for shearing.

Platypus skull

Elongated bill for grinding food

Platypus

DUCK'S BILL, MAMMAL'S FUR
The Australian platypus, a monotreme (egg-laying mammal) has a "bill" covered with leathery, sensitive skin. The bill is its only means of detecting food, by touch, as it forages in muddy creek beds. It closes its eyes and ears when diving.

LODGE IN THE RIVER
A beaver family lives in a semi-submerged mud-and-stick house called a "lodge". The beavers build a dam of branches, twigs, stones and mud across the stream, which raises the local water level and isolates the lodge for safety. During winter they swim under the ice to a "deep freezer" food cache of woody stems and twigs.

Lodge

Mud-and-stick walls

Living chamber (above water)

Food store

Raised water level

Dam

Entrance (under water)

*Long canine teeth
for grasping fish*

Otter skull

WATCHFUL SWIMMER
Nostrils, eyes and ears are placed
high on the head, so that the
otter can swim almost
submerged yet still
breathe, look and listen.

HUNTING THE OTTER
Otter hunting was once considered a sport, and still occurs in
some places, although in many countries this animal is now
protected by law. Today these creatures are also at risk from
development of waterways for angling and leisure pursuits,
and from pollution.

THE GAME OF LIFE
Otters spend much time
at play, either on their own
or with one another. Such "games"
may help to sharpen hunting skills.

*Molar teeth for
grinding food*

ENORMOUS GNAWERS
The beaver's large
chisel-like front teeth
(typical of rodents) can
gnaw through tree trunks
with ease.

NATURE'S LOGGERS
Beavers cut down trees for food
and also to build homes in lakes
they create for themselves
(below left). They eat
waterweeds, leaves
and other plant
matter.

*Large incisor teeth
for gnawing*

Beaver skull

Beaver

FLAT SLAP
The beaver's tail is flattened and scaly. Besides its use
as a rudder and paddle, it can be slapped onto
the water's surface to warn colleagues of danger.

Beaver tail

Frogs, toads and newts

AMPHIBIANS ARE ANIMALS that never quite set themselves free of the water. As their name suggests (*amphi* for "both", and *bios* for "life"), they lead a double-life: in the water when young, and out of it when adult. Many adult amphibians on land must stay in damp places so that they do not dry out. This is because some species "breathe" oxygen through the skin, as well as breathing it into their lungs, and only moist skin will absorb oxygen. Young amphibians just hatched from their eggs also absorb dissolved oxygen from the water through their skins, and in addition they have gills for breathing. Some amphibians, like the common frog and toad, prefer still water in which to breed. Others, such as the hellbender, a huge salamander from North America, frequent fast-flowing water. This may be because there is more dissolved oxygen in moving water than in still water, and such large amphibians need a copious supply. Amphibians are divided into two main groups, distinguished by their tails: newts and salamanders have them, while frogs and toads do not (except as tadpoles).

CLUMPED TOGETHER
Common frogs lay eggs (spawn) in clumps that float below the surface. Spawn from several females may collect in one large mass.

Common frog spawn

Developing tadpole

STRUNG OUT
The common toad's spawn forms a black-speckled jelly necklace, 2 m (6 ft) or more long, wrapped around plant stems.

PATCHY PATTERNING
Common frogs vary in colour, but in general they are mottled with patches of olive-green and brown.

Developing tadpole

Common toad spawn

Tiger salamander

WARNING COLOURATION
The vivid yellow and black blotchy pattern of the tiger salamander is thought to be a warning signal, advising potential predators that its skin and glands produce foul-tasting secretions.

Warning colouration

One-year-old common frog

Tympanum

Golden lined frog

GOLDEN LINED FROG
A frog's "ear" (tympanum) is a disc-shaped membrane behind its eye. That frogs have good hearing is indicated by the calls and croaks they use to communicate, especially when breeding.

Common toad

Unwebbed fore feet

Cuban tree frog

Rounded fingertips bear sticky pads

STICKY FINGERS
This Cuban tree frog has rounded, sticky pads on its digits, which help it grip leaves and twigs. Adults spend all their time in trees, leaving them only to lay their eggs in a pond.

DRESSED IN GREEN
The startlingly green skin of Australia's dwarf tree frog gives good concealment among the bright leaves of its forest home.

Dwarf tree frog

GOING FOR A WALK
The squat, heavily built common toad prefers to move by walking in an unhurried fashion, though it can leap a short way when at risk. The "toes" are webbed, the "fingers" are not.

Mottled skin for camouflage

Webbed hind feet

GREEN TOAD
The green toad is smaller and slimmer than the common toad and can run surprisingly fast. It is often confused with the natterjack toad.

Green toad

TIME TO GO
For spawning, natterjacks tend to choose shallow, temporary pools. In summer, crowds of toadlets prepare to leave the water.

Natterjack toadlets

Natterjack spawn

Developing tadpole

NATTERJACK SPAWN
A single row of eggs is laid, entwined in pebbles or plant stems.

SUBMARINE HUNTER
The palmate newt spends part of the year on land, hibernating or feeding at night on worms and other small animals. It returns to the pond in spring to court and lay eggs.

Palmate newt

A BIG EATER
All adult frogs and toads are carnivores. Big frogs have big mouths that can swallow large food items. There are several reliable reports of American bullfrogs eating bats!

American bullfrog

Mandarin newt

Developing newtlet

Newt eggs

Warning colouration

RED FOR DANGER!
Like the tiger salamander opposite, the mandarin newt has bright colours warning that it makes a foul mouthful. It lives in Asia.

SINGLE EGGS
Most newt species lay their eggs singly, attaching them to leaves and water-weeds. Some species wrap each egg carefully in a leaf for protection.

FABLED FROGS
Aesop wrote of the hare's dissatisfaction at being prey to so many animals. But when it saw the frog's plight, it felt less hard done by.

A FOAM NEST
The foam-nest tree frog whips up a bubbly nest, to keep the spawn moist. When grown, tadpoles drop into the pond beneath.

MATING
Early spring is a time of commotion in the pond, as amphibians gather to breed. The male common frog struggles with rivals to find a female, and then takes up a piggyback position. He may stay there for many days, clasping her slippery chest skin tightly with roughened pads on his thumbs. As the eggs are laid, he sheds sperm over them. The exhausted pair then part company.

MALE MIDWIFE
The midwife toad is in fact the "husband", who gathers the egg string and carries it around his back legs for up to a month. As the tadpoles begin to hatch he releases them into a pool.

This 18th-century engraving is an impression of how a male midwife toad carries its eggs

Hunters in the water

More than 300 million years ago, the reptiles appeared on Earth. They probably evolved from amphibians (pp. 38-9). Their big advantage was that they had made a complete break from an aquatic environment. Unlike amphibians, which needed water in which to lay their jelly-covered eggs, reptiles had hard-shelled eggs that could be laid on land. Soon, as dinosaurs, they would come to dominate life on land. Since that time, however, some groups of reptiles have made an "evolutionary U-turn" and gone back to life in the water. Many snakes readily take to water, swim well, and hunt fish, frogs, aquatic insects and land creatures that come to the pond or riverside for a drink. Indeed, certain groups of reptiles, such as crocodiles and turtles, have never really left the aquatic environment, though they come on to land to lay their eggs.

GIANT IN THE WATER
One of the longest, and certainly the heaviest, of snakes is the water boa, or anaconda, of northern South America. Lengths of 9 m (30 ft) and weights of over 200 kg (440 lb) have been recorded. It can consume creatures as large as a pig.

Water moccasin

DOWN IN THE SWAMPS
This old engraving shows the water moccasin, a venomous swamp dweller of the south eastern USA. When this snake is threatened it opens its mouth wide to reveal the white inside lining, hence its other name of "cottonmouth".

Viperine water snake

Zig-zag markings on the snake's back are similar to those of a common viper, or adder

Snake swims by undulations of its body

Turtle…or terrapin?

There is little biological distinction between a turtle and a terrapin. Most experts call the entire group (chelonians) turtles. Small, freshwater species may be named terrapins, from a North American Indian word that referred originally to the diamondback terrapin. But the numerous exceptions confuse the issue. Whatever our labels, however, many turtles are well equipped for an aquatic life, either in fresh water or in the sea. Some have webbed or flipper-like feet, and leathery skin overlying the shell on their underside, through which oxygen can be absorbed. They tend to be omnivores, taking aquatic animals, fruit from bankside trees, and carrion as they become available.

SCARCELY A RIPPLE

The viperine water snake of Europe is quite at home in the water, swimming easily across its surface. It will strike at virtually any suitably sized prey, from fish to frogs and even small mammals. Adults grow to 80 cm (2.5 ft) or more (this one is approximately life-sized, but young). Despite its name and its zig-zag markings reminiscent of the adder, it is not poisonous, being a relative of the grass snake.

Yellow-bellied terrapin

Distinctive brown and yellow markings

OPPOSITE FEET FORWARD

The yellow-bellied terrapin may walk along the bed of a river or lake, or swim by paddling alternately with two limbs - the front foot on one side and the back foot on the other.

Left-hand foreleg is forward when right-hand foreleg is back

Smooth plates on shell

Shell lacks bony plates

Soft-shelled turtle

Strong horny jaws in mouth

Webbed feet for swimming

Ridged bony plates on shell

THE SOFT SHELL

Soft-shelled turtles lack the hard, bony plates carried by the hard-shelled types. This life-size youngster will grow to about 30 cm (1 ft) long.

SNAPPY CUSTOMER

This young common snapper will reach almost 50 cm (20 in) when adult. Its strong, sharp-ridged jaws will be able to crack the shells of other turtles which form part of its diet.

Common snapper

Water snakes will eat all kinds of freshwater life, including this unfortunate frog

DIVING DRAGON

Eastern water dragons frequent watercourses in eastern Australia. This lizard is a powerful swimmer, using its vertically flattened tail and long legs. It has a body length of nearly 1 m (3 ft), a tail more than double this, and it eats all manner of water and shore life, from worms and frogs to shellfish, small mammals and fruit.

Eastern water dragon

Floating flowers

IN ANCIENT TIMES people were amazed to see that, when a previously dry watercourse filled with recent rains, the splendid blooms of water-lilies would soon appear.

Flowerbud

These aquatic plants gained a reputation as a symbol of immortality; the ancient Egyptians even worshipped one type of water-lily, the sacred lotus. Water-lily flowers are made more mysterious by their daily routine: they remain closed during the morning, open to reveal their beauty at around noon, and towards evening close again and perhaps sink slightly into the water. On overcast days they might not open fully at all. This may be an adaptation to aid pollination by flying insects, which are more likely to be active in the afternoon's warmth. During dull weather, signifying wind and rain, the closed flowers are less likely to be swamped. The flowers and leaves grow on tough, rubbery stems - 3 m (10 ft) long in some species - anchored in the mud on the beds of ponds, lakes and slow rivers.

THE "BEAUTIFUL NUISANCE"
The water hyacinth is a free-floating flowering plant which spreads rapidly, often clogging rivers, canals and ditches.

Red hybrid - "Escarboucle"

Leaves may be heart-shaped, oval or round

Yellow water-lily leaves are patterned with a red tinge

White water-lily flower

Leathery leaves repel water droplets

Pink hybrid

Conspicuous yellow stamens

LILIES AND THEIR HYBRIDS

There are some 60 species of water-lily around the world (in some areas they are known as lotuses). Their beautiful waxy-looking flowers and bold circular leaves have made them favourites in ponds, ornamental water gardens and landscaped lakes. Horticulturalists have bred many differently coloured flowers.

Yellow hybrid - "Chromatella"

Waxy petals

Pink hybrid

FLOATING SAUCERS

Some of the largest leaves of any plant belong to the Amazonian water lily. A single leaf may be more than 1.5 m (5 ft) across, with an upturned rim and stiff reinforcing ribs beneath.

LILY LEAF CASE

The china mark moth's caterpillar cuts out an oval of leaf, fastening it to the underside with silk thread to form a protective case.

Water-lily leaf

WELL-USED LEAVES

The leaves (lily "pads") are used by many water creatures. Pond snails browse on them and lay their speckled, jelly-sausage egg masses (p. 8) on their undersides. Frogs rest on or under them, waiting to snap up unwary insects. In some places the pads grow so densely that certain creatures can walk on them. A bird, the African jacana, has long, widespread toes and is known as the "lily trotter", as it steps delicately on the leaves in its search for insects and seeds.

Plants at the pond's surface

MANY WATER PLANTS are not rooted in the mud at the bottom of the pond, but are free to float over the surface of the water. Most have trailing roots that balance the plant and absorb minerals, although some have no roots at all. At first sight, these plants seem to have few problems. Unlike some land plants, they are well supported and, out in the middle of the pond, they cannot be shaded by trees or taller plants. But there are disadvantages: the water's surface can be whipped by the wind into waves that drag and tear at them; rain might collect on a leaf and sink it, or the leaf may be frozen underwater!

SMALLEST PLANTS
The duckweeds are among the smallest and simplest flowering plants in the world. Flowers are only produced in shallow water that receives plenty of sunlight. The "leaves" contain air-filled spaces called lacunae that keep them afloat.

Tiny roots absorb minerals from the water

Blanket weed

Duckweed

Surface view

Three of the many species of duckweed are shown here

Side view

Pale-green mass is made up of hundreds of thread-like plants

New plants produced by side-shoots that break off and float away

A GREEN BLANKET
"Blanket weed" is a popular name for the green hair-like masses of algae that burst into growth in the spring. These plants can spread so quickly that they cover the surface like a blanket of green cotton-wool, blocking out light to the plants below·

Water-lily leaf and flowerbud (pp. 42-3)

Two new leaves developing from old leaf

Ivy-leaved duckweed

CIRCLE OF STRENGTH
Like many other floating leaves, those of water-lilies have a rounded outline. This design probably helps to prevent tearing, when wind ruffles the pond surface. The shiny upper surface repels rainwater so that the leaves are not swamped by a shower. Lilies are not true floating plants because they are rooted in the mud (pp. 42-3).

FLOWERING FLOATER
This engraving shows another species of duckweed that floats on the water surface only when it is flowering, otherwise it floats just under the water surface. The ivy-leaf shape is formed when two new leaves develop, one on each side of the original leaf.

Azolla water fern

Pink tinge develops to deep red in autumn

Thread-like roots trail beneath the plant

FLOATING FRONDS
Azolla is not a flowering plant but a fern, so technically its delicately sculptured "leaves" are called fronds. Tiny hairs repel water and prevent the fronds becoming waterlogged and sinking.

Leaves are similar in shape to water-lily leaves

WINTER SEEDS AND BUDS
Frogbit, a relative of water soldier (below), has a similar technique for avoiding the ice and frost of winter. In this case, however, the parts that overwinter are the seeds and the specially grown, dense "winter buds". Both are produced in the autumn and sink to rest in the mud, until the increasing light levels and temperatures of spring spur them into growth, when they float to the surface again. In summer, the delicate white flowers and kidney-shaped leaves carpet whole ponds and ditches.

Frogbit

Plants will sometimes root in shallow water

Water soldier

Trailing roots

GREEN ROSETTES
The rosettes of water soldier spend summer floating at or near the pond surface. As autumn approaches, the leaves develop a slimy coating that weighs them down. The plant sinks, to avoid winter's frost and ice. Fresh spring leaves buoy it up again. This plant reproduces by sending out runners that root at a distance, and by male and female flowers borne on separate plants.

WATER SOLDIER IN FLOWER
White flowers are produced in midsummer, male and female flowers on different plants. Once flowering is over, the plant sinks to the bottom of the pond.

Long, unbranched roots hang down under the plant to balance it

Underwater weeds

Submerged weeds grow in ponds and rivers like trees in a miniature underwater forest. They provide shelter for some animals, and places of ambush for others which dash-and-grab unwary victims swimming by. They are food for many creatures, from pond snails to ducks. They also provide that most vital substance, oxygen. As a plant carries out photosynthesis, capturing the sun's light energy to build new tissues, it produces oxygen as a by-product. The oxygen diffuses into the water and is used by both plants and animals for the process of respiration. On a sunny day, small bubbles of oxygen can be seen coating underwater plants and occasionally rising to the surface.

Rigid hornwort

CURTAIN OF ROOTS
The water violet's abundant roots hang like a veil in the water. The stem grows out of the water, where it bears not leaves but pale, pinky, five-petalled flowers.

Water violet

TOTAL SUBMERSION
Feathery-looking hornworts are completely at home in the water. Even the flowers are submerged, growing at the junction of the leaf and the stem.

New Zealand pygmyweed

GREEN BALL
Volvox is a microscopic water plant and an important food for tiny creatures.

Trailing roots

Canadian waterweed

NEW ZEALAND PYGMYWEED
This plant is causing concern in many waterways because of its uncontrolled spread. It was first introduced as an aquarium oxygenator.

ACROSS THE ATLANTIC
Canadian waterweed left its North American home in about 1840, soon colonizing and clogging up European ponds and rivers.

POND "PLANKTON"
At 25X magnification, the microscopic world of underwater plants is revealed.

PERCH IN THE GRASS
Tape grass is one of the popularly named "river" grasses. It offers a hideout for fish, particularly the perch, camouflaged by its vertical stripes (p. 23).

Tape grass

Narrow leaves resemble the needles of a fir tree

Bulbous rush

SLENDER WATERWEED
The pale-green water starwort sways in clumps in the water.

FLUSHED RUSH
The bulbous rush is usually rooted on the pondside, but sometimes it grows underwater, becoming very elongated.

Water starwort

Dragonflies and damselflies

THESE LARGE, POWERFUL FLIERS speed to and fro along the bank and over the water's surface, searching out their food of small airborne creatures with their enormous eyes. Like those of other insects, the dragonfly's eyes are made up of many separate lenses that probably give a mosaic-like picture of the world. As the adults dart about above, the water-dwelling nymphs crawl on the pond bottom. Like their parents, they seize and eat any small creature they can catch, from other water insects to tadpoles and fish.

Damselflies

These are smaller and more slender relatives of dragonflies. Although at first glance they appear very similar in shape and lifestyle, there are several important differences that distinguish them from the dragonflies - most obviously the fact that the damselfly holds its two pairs of wings together over its back when resting, while the dragonfly holds them out flat at the sides of its body.

SIMILAR WINGS
A damselfly's wings are roughly equal in size, with rounded ends, unlike the dragonfly's wings.

Emerald damselfly

Eyes protrude from side of head

Rounded wing tips

Blue-tailed damselfly

MALE AND FEMALE
In most damselflies, the female has a slightly wider and less colourful abdomen than the male.

Azure damselfly

Large red damselfly

WEAK FLIERS
Damselflies tend to be weaker fliers than their dragonfly cousins.

SMALLER EYES
The small eyes of the damselfly are set on the sides of the head, while dragonflies' eyes meet at the top of the head.

Cast nymphal skin

Broad-bodied libellula nymph

Young southern hawker nymph

Mask — — *Hooks on mask impale prey* — — *Mask*

THE DEADLY MASK
Dragonfly nymphs are the scourge of the pond, eating anything they can catch with their "mask". This is a horny flap, equivalent to the lower lip, which has two vicious hooks at the end (above). Normally the mask is folded under the head, but it is hinged so that it can suddenly shoot out to impale prey, which is then pulled back to the mouth.

CAST-OFF CLOTHING
This perfectly detailed empty skin is from a brown hawker dragonfly's final moult. New adults usually emerge at night or early in the morning, to avoid predators.

THE MATING GAME
The male dragonfly clasps the female and she bends to pick up the sperm from a special organ at the front of his abdomen.

THE LIFE OF THE DRAGONFLY
A dragonfly begins life as an egg laid in water. It hatches into a larva that grows by splitting its skin and forming a new, larger skin. There are between eight and 15 moults over two years or more, depending on the species. A gradual change to adult form like this (compared with a sudden change, for example caterpillar to butterfly) is called "incomplete metamorphosis", and the intermediate larval stages are referred to as "nymphs". Finally the nymph climbs up a stem into the air, splits its skin a final time, and the adult emerges.

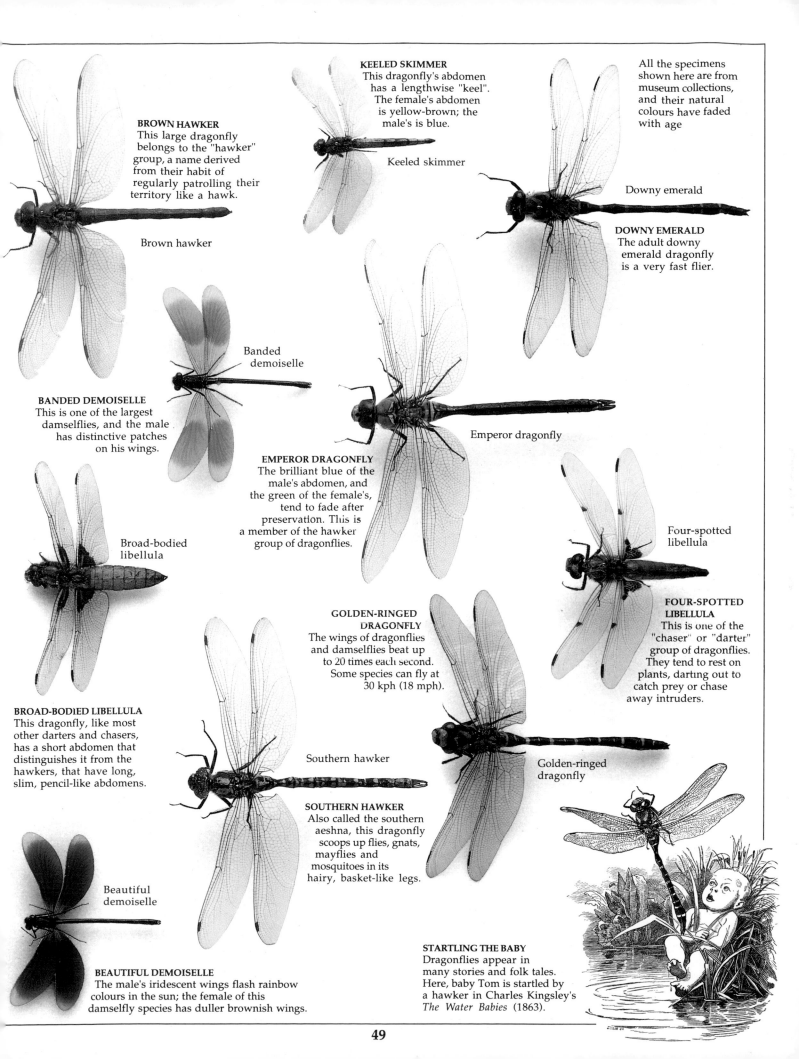

BROWN HAWKER
This large dragonfly belongs to the "hawker" group, a name derived from their habit of regularly patrolling their territory like a hawk.

Brown hawker

KEELED SKIMMER
This dragonfly's abdomen has a lengthwise "keel". The female's abdomen is yellow-brown; the male's is blue.

Keeled skimmer

All the specimens shown here are from museum collections, and their natural colours have faded with age

Downy emerald

DOWNY EMERALD
The adult downy emerald dragonfly is a very fast flier.

Banded demoiselle

BANDED DEMOISELLE
This is one of the largest damselflies, and the male has distinctive patches on his wings.

Broad-bodied libellula

EMPEROR DRAGONFLY
The brilliant blue of the male's abdomen, and the green of the female's, tend to fade after preservation. This is a member of the hawker group of dragonflies.

Emperor dragonfly

Four-spotted libellula

FOUR-SPOTTED LIBELLULA
This is one of the "chaser" or "darter" group of dragonflies. They tend to rest on plants, darting out to catch prey or chase away intruders.

GOLDEN-RINGED DRAGONFLY
The wings of dragonflies and damselflies beat up to 20 times each second. Some species can fly at 30 kph (18 mph).

BROAD-BODIED LIBELLULA
This dragonfly, like most other darters and chasers, has a short abdomen that distinguishes it from the hawkers, that have long, slim, pencil-like abdomens.

Southern hawker

Golden-ringed dragonfly

SOUTHERN HAWKER
Also called the southern aeshna, this dragonfly scoops up flies, gnats, mayflies and mosquitoes in its hairy, basket-like legs.

Beautiful demoiselle

BEAUTIFUL DEMOISELLE
The male's iridescent wings flash rainbow colours in the sun; the female of this damselfly species has duller brownish wings.

STARTLING THE BABY
Dragonflies appear in many stories and folk tales. Here, baby Tom is startled by a hawker in Charles Kingsley's *The Water Babies* (1863).

49

Insects in the water

Insects, the most adaptable creatures on earth, can live in places ranging from glaciers to hot springs, and deserts to tropical forests. About half of the 25 major groups of insects live in fresh water. Some, such as water beetles and bugs, spend nearly all their lives in water. Others, like mayflies and caddis flies, have a watery "childhood" and emerge into the air when adult. Certain aquatic insects, including the water beetles, are air-breathing and visit the surface regularly to obtain supplies, which they store by various ingenious means (p. 51). Others have specialized "gills" to extract oxygen from the water, while still others can absorb sufficent dissolved oxygen through their skin.

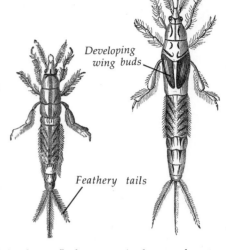

Developing wing buds

Feathery tails

Like dragonfly larvae (p. 48), mayfly larvae are called nymphs

As the nymph matures, small "wing buds" grow with each moult

Rat-tailed maggots (drone fly larvae)

Adult drone fly

MAGGOT'S PARENT
The rat-tailed maggot is the larva of the drone fly, a type of hoverfly, named for its resemblance to the drones of the honey bee.

Breathing tube

Adult mayfly

Long "tails" identify this insect

SPRING FEAST
Mayfly adults emerge in huge swarms in spring. They fly weakly, have no mouths and so cannot feed, and spend their few days of adult life mating and laying eggs by dipping their abdomens in water. The "dance of the mayflies" attracts hungry fish - and anglers, who use mayfly lures to catch trout.

MAGGOT WITH SNORKEL *above*
The rat-tailed maggot has a long breathing tube of three sections that telescope into one another. It lives in the mud of shallow ponds, sucking up decaying food.

THREE-TAILED FLY
Like its larvae, the adult mayfly has three very distinctive trailing "tails". Mayflies are known as "spinners" by anglers.

GROWN-UP CADDIS
Adult caddis flies are less well-known than their water-dwelling youngsters. The adults are drab grey or brown, come out at dusk or night, and are easily confused with small moths. They flit about near water, rarely feed, and seldom live more than a few days.

Adult caddis flies

Wings covered with fine hairs

Antennae often as long as the body

STICKS AND STONES
Many species of caddis fly have aquatic larvae that build protective cases around themselves. The construction material is characteristic of each species. As the larva grows, it adds more material to the front of the case.

Larval cases may be attached to water plants or lie on the pond bottom

Plant stalks

Discarded snail shells

Small stones

Case is extended by adding material to the front end

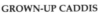

Head of larva emerges from case to feed

Every species makes a distinctive case

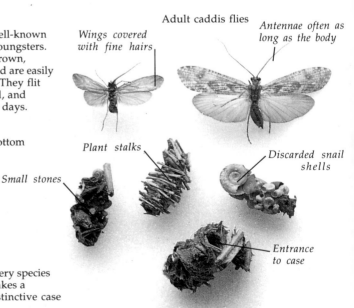

Entrance to case

Cases built by caddis-fly larvae

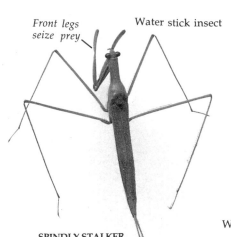

Front legs seize prey

Water stick insect

Front legs catch tadpoles and other prey

Water scorpion

Breathing tube

Water scorpion

Pond skater

Rowing legs

Steering legs

SPINDLY STALKER
The water stick insect grabs any small underwater creature with its mantis-like front legs, and then sucks the juices from inside, using its needle-shaped mouthparts. A short trip to the surface allows fresh supplies of air to be sucked through the long tail, the two parts of which are usually held together by bristles to form a tube.

Parts of breathing tube

STING IN THE TAIL?
No, the "tail" of the water scorpion is a harmless breathing tube, unlike the poisonous version of its dry-land namesake. The dangerous parts are the powerful claw-like front legs and stinging beak-shaped mouth.

DEAD LEAF?
When disturbed, the water scorpion sinks to the bottom and stays still, looking like a dead leaf. This is a smaller species.

WATER-WALKER
The back four feet of the pond skater have thick pads of hair that repel water, so preventing this bug from sinking as it rows across the surface of the pond.

Wing covers

Backswimmer

BACKSWIMMER . . .
A bug not a beetle, this unusual top view of a backswimmer shows its hard wing cases that cover strong flying wings. Most of its time, however, is spent hanging upside-down below the water surface.

Water boatman

Hair-covered legs for swimming

WATER BOATMAN
This insect's name refers to the oar-like rowing motions of its legs as it propels itself through the water. It eats any plant debris or algae it can grub up or catch in its sieve-like front legs.

Air bubble

THE BUBBLE CHAMBER
The air-breathing water spider (not actually an insect, but an arachnid), makes a "diving bell" to live in. It weaves a web among water plants and stocks it with air from the surface (below). The air being transported in its body hairs gives the spider's abdomen a silvery sheen (left).

BEETLE POWER
In a small pond, the great diving beetle has few predators, but many prey - insects, tadpoles and small fish such as this unlucky stickleback.

SPARE AIR
Water beetles are air-breathing insects and have devised clever methods for collecting air from the surface. Many aquatic beetles trap air on the hairs under the body. Others trap air under their wing cases, making them buoyant and always struggling to swim downwards. Some, like the silver water beetle shown here, use both methods.

Silver water beetle

Freshwater shells

Aᴌᴌ ᴛʜᴇ ʟɪꜰᴇ-ꜱɪᴢᴇᴅ ꜱʜᴇʟʟꜱ shown here have two features in common: their builder-owners live in fresh water, and they belong to the mollusc group. The mollusc's shell is made chiefly of calcium-containing minerals such as calcium carbonate (lime). To make its shell, the animal must absorb minerals from the water. In general, aquatic molluscs are more common in hard-water areas, where water is naturally richer in dissolved minerals. The snails and limpets (gastropods) are mostly grazers, on water plants and the algal "scum" on submerged stones, although some species can filter-feed. The mussels and cockles (bivalves) feed by sucking in a stream of water and filtering out tiny food particles.

How do molluscs breathe?

Water snails are divided into two groups, depending on how they breathe. The great pond snail, ramshorn snail and bladder snail are known as pulmonates - they breathe air, like land snails. They float up to the surface, open a breathing aperture and take a gulp of air into a lung-like cavity. The other group, including valve, river and spire snails, are called prosobranchs. They breathe by absorbing oxygen from the water through gills.

SEVEN SEASONS
The growth rings on this swan mussel's shell show that it is about six or seven years old.

DUCK MUSSEL
This bivalve's shell is more swollen than that of the swan mussel.

RIGHT-HANDERS
Usually great pond snail shells curl to the right, but "left-handers" are known.

SEE-THROUGH SNAIL
The nautilus ramshorn is so small that its shell is semi-transparent.

BIVALVE LARDER
Pea mussels are the staple food of many fish and water birds.

WANDERING SNAIL
The whorls of this wandering snail are compressed at its tip.

CURLY WHORLY
The tightly coiled white ramshorn is from ponds and streams.

MARBLED SNAIL
The nerite snail has an attractively stippled and whorled shell.

JOINTED SHELL
The horny pea cockle is a bivalve mollusc as it has two shells.

River shellfish

The molluscs below and left (swan and duck mussels) tend to frequent flowing water, compared to the still waters of ponds and lakes. The growth rings of the mussels indicate their age, which might be up to a dozen years for a large individual. Growth rings can be seen on snails too, but they are less clearly divided into a year-by-year pattern.

Snails grow by adding new material at the open end of the shell

TWISTING TUBE
Snail shells are coiled, gradually widening tubes, clearly seen on this Lister's river snail.

MINERAL COLLECTOR
River snail's shells may be over 5 cm (2 in) long - a lot of calcium to collect.

LISTENING SNAIL
The ear pond snail's flared opening resembles a human ear.

SWOLLEN JOINT
This tumid unio mussel has an inflated "umbo" near its hinge-line.

ZEBRA MUSSEL
This bivalve is anchored to rocks by sticky byssus threads.

WATERWEED EATER
The great ramshorn water snail browses on underwater plants.

DISTINCTIVE SHELL
The last whorl on the bladder snail's shell is large compared to the other whorls.

STUBBY AND SHINY
These shiny, compact shells belong to the common bithynia.

BITHYNIA LEACHI
These bithynias have no common name; only a scientific name.

STRAIGHT SNAIL
The river limpet is a true snail, but its shell is not coiled.

OPEN AND SHUT
The "valve" of the valve snail is the door or operculum, of its shell.

SLOW WATER
The lake limpet can often be found in slow-flowing rivers.

OPENING THE DOOR
The operculum, or door, to the shell allows the snail to emerge to feed.

Operculum makes a watertight seal to shell when closed

TWO TINY SHELLS
Pea cockles are tiny, filter-feeding bivalve molluscs.

SALTY AND FRESH
Jenkin's spire shells are found in estuaries as well as in ponds and rivers.

Head of the river

Many rivers begin life as fast-flowing upland streams, cascading across moors or through craggy woodlands. The deep, rocky gulleys, the overhanging trees and the splashing waters create contrasting worlds: shady, damp banks with lush green vegetation, and streambeds where rushing water washes away nearly all plant life and any but the most tenaciously clinging animals. In a flood, entire plant and animal communities may be swept away. Yet new seeds and spores soon spring up, while creatures creep out from under rocks to fight their way back upstream.

Dipper

UNDERWATER WALKER
The dipper bobs its head as it stands on midstream rocks, watching for small animal prey. It can also walk along the river bed, head facing upstream and tail acting as a hydroplane in the current, to keep its feet firmly on the bottom.

ARMOURED CRAYFISH
Hard water is favoured by the freshwater crayfish, a relative of the marine lobster. It needs plenty of calcium minerals to build its shell.

BANKSIDE MOISTURE-LOVERS
Succulent growths of mosses, liverworts, ferns and other damp-loving plants colonize the banks and splash-zone rocks. The larger heart-shaped leaves are marsh violet.

Hard outer shell made up from minerals in the water

Freshwater crayfish

Polytrichum moss

Fern

Puffball

Liverwort

YOUNG BALL
Fungi, such as this young member of the puffball group, relish shady streamside conditions.

LICHEN BRANCH
Shady, damp conditions are ideal for certain lichens, which are co-operative combinations of fungi and algae. Two different kinds of leafy lichen are growing on this branch.

Great woodrush

Liverwort

Marsh violet

Bullhead

UPSTREAM FISH
Despite the fast current fish, such as the bullhead, are found at the head of the river. The bullhead's flattened shape allows it to hide under stones.

Oak leaves

FOOD FROM ABOVE
Trees such as the oak hang
over the water, and their fruits
and leaves provide sustenance
for river-dwellers if they
fall into the water.

Fontinalis
moss

Acorns

*Galls caused by insects
living in oak leaves*

*Deeply divided
fronds*

Great woodrush

BETWEEN THE BOULDERS
Groups of midstream boulders
often support a thriving
island of life; here, great
woodrush sprouts from
current-collected soil.

UNDERWATER MOSS
Fontinalis or "willow moss" undulates with
the current in slower streams and rivers,
anchored to a stone or fallen log.

*Shiny,
undivided
fronds*

*Rows of
spores*

*Layer of moss
growing on
boulders*

Male fern

FEATHERY FRONDS
Many types of ferns thrive in the
shaded, humid conditions along
riverbanks. The hart's-tongue
fern (far right) has rib-like
rows of brown spore cases
on the undersides of its fronds.
It is unusual among ferns
in having solid,
unbranched fronds.

*Feathery,
pale-green
fronds*

*Shiny,
dark-green
fronds*

Hard
fern

Lady fern

Hart's-tongue
fern

Brown spore cases

55

Life along the riverbank

As STREAMS BECOME MORE SEDATE, and their courses join up and widen, the river comes into being. But when does a stream become a river? One definition is that streams are less than 5 m (15 ft) wide, while rivers are more. Larger rivers usually have a slower current, allowing rooted plants to flourish at the water's edge. Whatever the distinction, riverbank life suits many kinds of plants and animals. On a high-banked river, the soil at the water's edge is nearly always saturated, but it becomes drier higher up the bank. So there is often a characteristic zonation of plant life, with mud-rooted irises and water plantains lower down, and the damp-ground hemp agrimony, balsam and similar flowers slightly higher.

Thistle-shaped flowerhead

ABOUT TO FLOWER
This teasel's flower is just emerging, its pinkish-mauve petals not yet visible.

FIVE IN ONE
Each small "flower" of hemp agrimony is a cluster of five even smaller "florets".

Teasel

Hooks attach fruits to passing animals

Spiny flowerhead is still developing

Heart-shaped leaves are slightly downy

Messing about on the river has long been a favourite leisure pursuit

Explosive seed cases are developing inside the flowers

Hemp agrimony

HITCHING A RIDE
Young great burdock flowers already bear the hooks that, when the seeds ripen, will catch on fur, coats and socks.

Leaves have toothed edges

TRAVELLING FLOWER
Indian, or Himalayan, balsam, a native of that region, is a greenhouse escapee. It has spread along many riverbanks, ditch sides and damp gulleys.

Leaves have serrated margins

Stem has reddish tinge

Indian balsam
(Himalayan balsam)

HIGH-WATER MARK
The river's spring flood left surface debris stuck onto this overhanging twig, 1 m (3 ft) above summer's water level.

Old plant stalks caught round twig

RIVERBANK HOME
Many mammals use the riverbank as a home. Otters live in well-hidden "holts" in the bank vegetation or under over-hanging tree roots.

The pyramidal inflorescences make water plantain a dramatic plant on the riverbank

Water plantain leaf

Flatworm

DOWN IN THE MUD
The beds of ponds and rivers abound with small creatures such as these, which are food for fish and other creatures.

Freshwater shrimp

The caddis larva has built its case from tiny pebbles (p. 50)

Flatworm

Freshwater shrimp

Loaches

BARBEL-BEARD
The barbels, or "whiskers", of the loach are used as feeling organs. This river dweller emerges from under stones after dusk to forage in the mud for worms, insects and other small water life.

Water starwort provides cover for these shy fish

Water plantain inflorescence

Toothmarks of mammal

AFTERNOON OPENING
Water plantain roots in the mud at the edges of small rivers. Its flowers are closed for most of the morning and evening, and open only after noon.

Tiny lilac flowers

Tiny molluscs attached to stone

Yellow flag leaves

CLAMPING DOWN
Under their rounded shells, the "feet" of these tiny freshwater molluscs grasp this rock firmly.

ANONYMOUS NIBBLER
These yellow flag leaves from a steep riverbank have been nibbled by a mammalian forager.

The river's mouth

THE RIVER'S COURSE is ended. Its banks curl out to become the seashore, and the tidal influx of salt water begins to impose itself on the plant and animal life. The last stretch of a river is known as the estuary, and it is here that the river's currents slow down to a crawl and the smallest mud and silt particles, still in suspension, slowly settle on the bed and banks. The water, mixed by waves and tides, is often cloudy so submerged plants are rare, since they do not receive enough light for photosynthesis (p. 10). Relatively few plants and animals are adapted to the enormous variations in salt concentration, but those that are face little competition and so are often found in huge numbers. The specimens shown below were all collected from an estuary, to give some idea of the range of animals and plants that can be found at the mouth of the river.

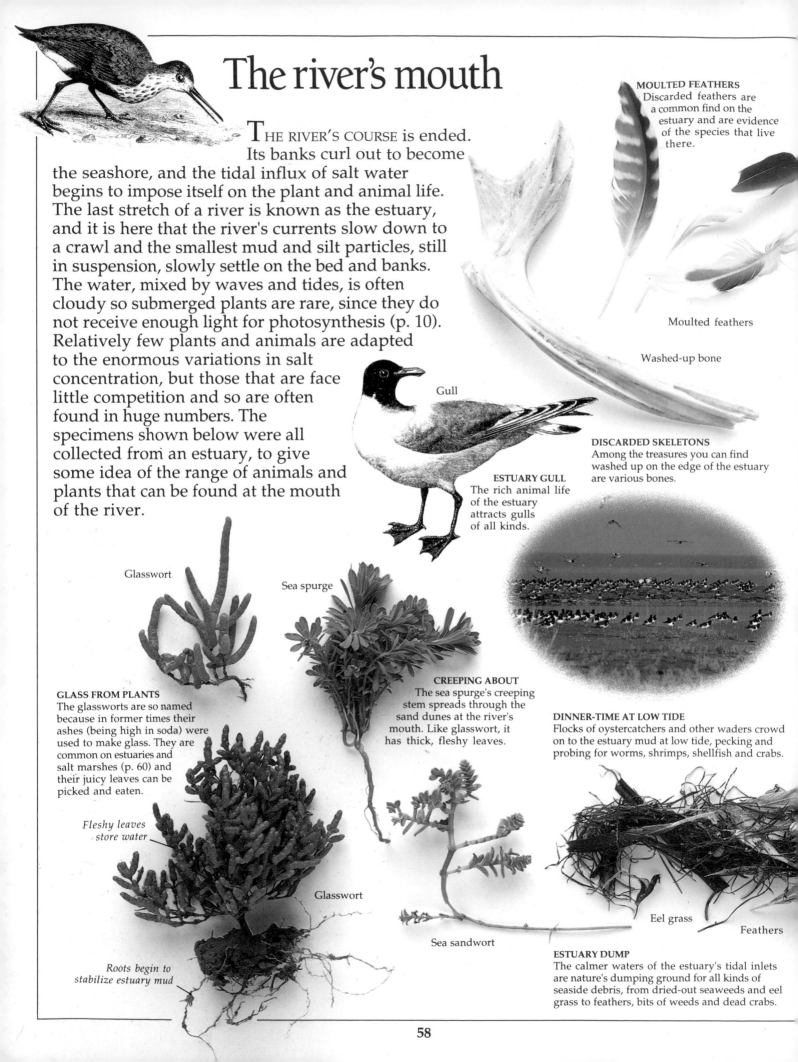

MOULTED FEATHERS
Discarded feathers are a common find on the estuary and are evidence of the species that live there.

Moulted feathers

Washed-up bone

Gull

ESTUARY GULL
The rich animal life of the estuary attracts gulls of all kinds.

DISCARDED SKELETONS
Among the treasures you can find washed up on the edge of the estuary are various bones.

Glasswort

Sea spurge

GLASS FROM PLANTS
The glassworts are so named because in former times their ashes (being high in soda) were used to make glass. They are common on estuaries and salt marshes (p. 60) and their juicy leaves can be picked and eaten.

CREEPING ABOUT
The sea spurge's creeping stem spreads through the sand dunes at the river's mouth. Like glasswort, it has thick, fleshy leaves.

DINNER-TIME AT LOW TIDE
Flocks of oystercatchers and other waders crowd on to the estuary mud at low tide, pecking and probing for worms, shrimps, shellfish and crabs.

Fleshy leaves store water

Glasswort

Sea sandwort

Eel grass

Feathers

Roots begin to stabilize estuary mud

ESTUARY DUMP
The calmer waters of the estuary's tidal inlets are nature's dumping ground for all kinds of seaside debris, from dried-out seaweeds and eel grass to feathers, bits of weeds and dead crabs.

A LOT TO LEARN
Oystercatcher chicks hatch from eggs laid in open or short vegetation around the estuary. The chicks can take up to 26 weeks to learn the specialized feeding techniques from their parents.

Tellin

Winkles

Cockle

Periwinkle

Mussel

Young crab

Oyster shell

Tellin shell

Cockle shell

Hole pecked by bird

Cockle shell

Tellin shell

HOLE IN ONE
These mollusc shells have been pecked through by estuary birds and the animal inside has been eaten.

Oystercatcher and chick

UNDER THE BREAKWATER
Any "obstruction" on the flat estuary, such as a breakwater or pier, soon becomes colonized by a variety of life that can withstand the fluctuating salinity. The sea slater is a crustacean, cousin of the woodlouse, and also a relative of the crab.

Sea slater

Lugworm

SHORE WORM
Squiggly casts on the estuary mud mark the position of a lugworm's U-shaped burrow.

Oyster shell

Shelduck and chick

Barnacles

Slipper limpet

Cockle shell

Razor shell

IN FROM THE SEA
The shells of true seashore molluscs are often washed up on the estuary shore, as was the small barnacle-encrusted stone, loosened by a storm.

SHELDUCK DUCKLING
Young shelducks look like most other ducklings, while the adult more resembles a goose. This waterfowl eats not only shellfish but also fish, worms and other small animals.

Crab

Pipefish

PIPEFISH
This relative of the seahorse has hardened outer skin and moves mainly using its dorsal fin. It copes well in the fluctuating salinity of estuary water.

Spiral wrack

SHORE WEED
In the more sheltered and seaward sites, shore algae can gain a foothold. This spiral wrack is characteristic of the upper shore zone.

The salt marsh

MANY ESTUARIES (p. 58) are flanked by a broad expanse of land, riddled with creeks and channels, the salty soil supporting its own, very distinctive, plant population. This is the salt marsh, and it is a very forbidding habitat for plants. Twice each day, sea water pours through the drainage channels and its salt soaks into the soil and mud. As the tide retreats, evaporation leaves behind a salty residue. Spring tides flood the entire marsh with sea water. Yet a few hours later, at low tide, heavy rain may have turned the surface into an almost freshwater habitat. The plants growing on a salt marsh have become specially adapted to such fluctuating conditions.

Flowerhead

PINKS AND PURPLES
Many salt-marsh plants have pink, lavender or purple flowers, colouring the whole marsh when in bloom. They tend to flower later in summer or in the autumn.

MARSH GRASS
The flowerheads of couch grass show in this clump of grasses from the higher, drier part of the marsh.

Sea aster

PLAIN PLANTAIN
The inconspicuous sea plantain populates the flat expanses of the salt marsh.

Flowerspike

Sea plantain

PURPLE AND YELLOW
In late summer and early autumn, the distinctive flowers of sea aster carpet large expanses of salt marsh.

Flower stalk arises from clump of fleshy leaves

SEA-LAVENDER
In late summer the flowers of the sea-lavender turn the salt marsh lilac.

Flower-spike

Couch grass

Leaves have a bluish tinge

SEA ARROW GRASS
Look among the grassy stems of the marsh and you will find the succulent stems of sea arrow grass. Despite its name, it is not a true grass.

Sea arrow grass

Sea-lavender

SILVER-GREEN LEAVES
The silvery leaves are covered with minute air-filled protective scales. Sea purslane grows along the edges of the channels and creeks within the salt marsh.

Ripening seedheads

Sea purslane

Leaves take up or lose water as the salinity changes

Thick roots

FLESHY LEAVES
The thick, fleshy leaves of salt-marsh dwellers are well demonstrated by this annual seablite.

Succulent leaves store water

BINDING IN THE MARSH
Cord grass, an early colonizer of the bare mud, is often planted on the lower parts of marshes and estuaries, to stabilize them with its underground stems and thick root system.

Annual seablite

The leaves secrete salt crystals to rid the plant of excess salt

Cord grass

RICH PICKINGS
Knots and other wading birds probe the mud of salt marsh channels for food.

Glasswort

Swollen, jointed stems store water

SALT-MARSH STABILIZER
Glasswort is one of the first plants to colonize the estuary mud, its delicate roots beginning the stabilizing process.

TIDAL DEBRIS
Each tide sweeps old stems, bits of crabs and other sundry debris along the channels that riddle the marsh.

SQUELCHING OOZE
This is the stuff of life in the salt marsh and estuary - glutinous, shiny mud, rich in organic matter.

Salt-marsh mud

Roots bind the slippery mud

Crabs

Empty shells

CAST-UP REMAINS
Young shore crabs, young cockles and a whelk's spongy, empty egg case are some of the items found when "marsh-combing" along the channel edges.

Whelk egg case

Study and conservation

THE FASCINATING WILDLIFE OF PONDS AND RIVERS is suffering in our modern world. Pollution, demand for housing or farming land, and more people using the water for relaxation and recreation are all taking their toll. Conserving and preserving our natural freshwater habitats is increasingly important. It begins with study and understanding. Students of nature are interested in what lives where, and why – and through observation rather than interference. When out on a field trip they have respect for nature, follow the country code, and obey the wildlife laws. If you wish to become involved in pond and river conservation, find out which organizations work in your local area.

THE MICROSCOPIC WORLD
A drop of pond water may look clear, but under a microscope such as this, it will be teeming with tiny water plants and animals. Magnification of about 20X to 200X is most common.

Magnifying glasses

LOOKING THROUGH LENSES
Magnifiers enable you to identify small water creatures or examine a flower's structure. A 10X lens is about right.

Field guide

Note pad

Screw-top glass jars

SHORT-STAY HOMES
Screw-top glass jars are useful for temporary storage and examination. Do not leave animals and plants in them for long.

SPOON AND BRUSH
These pieces of equipment enable small, delicate plants and animals to be transferred for study, and then replaced without harm.

DISHES AND DROPPERS
These allow small items to be moved gently and studied without too much disturbance.

Plastic spoons

FIELD NOTES
Note pad and field guide are vital. A pencil will not blot and can be sharpened carefully with a pocket knife.

Glass dish

Dropper

FARM WASTE
Accidental spillage of pig slurry into this river killed chub, dace, roach - and thousands of smaller animals.

Waterproof camera

DAMP-PROOF SNAPS
Modern waterproof cameras allow photographs to be taken in the wettest places, even in the spray of a fast stream. Photos record nature without disturbing it.

The dangers of pollution

Ponds, rivers and other freshwater habitats are under constant threat of pollution. Fertilizers, pesticides and other farming chemicals are washed through the soil by rain and into watercourses, where they may adversely affect the balance of nature. Industrial wastes discharged from factories into rivers can damage water life for long stretches downstream. Most authorities have clean-water laws, but these are not always observed; "accidents" happen, and inspectors cannot monitor every backwater. We can all contribute, by reporting suspicions to the authorities, or by volunteering to help clean out and restock a weed-choked pond, or by clearing a stream used as a rubbish tip.

Folding
pocket
knife

Plastic bags
and ties

Fine-mesh sieve

Secateurs

WATER-PROOFING
Aquatic plants dry out
quickly in air. Keep them
wet during transit in
plastic bags.

A CLEAN CUT
Take plant samples only with permission,
and with a sharp blade for minimum damage.

Fork

Trowel

SIEVE FOR SORTING
A fine-mesh sieve can
be rocked gently in
water to sort small
animals from mud
and silt.

TAKING A SAMPLE
A bucket on a string
can be tossed from a
bridge, bank or boat
to sample the water.

Sealable plastic containers

SPLASH-PROOF CONTAINERS
Pack animals carefully in
sealable containers, using
waterweed as "padding"
to minimize splashing.

Large-mesh net

SMALL DIGGERS
If you are permitted to dig up plants
or search for muddy-bottom
creatures, use a clean, sharp
fork or trowel and take
great care.

Water-sampling
bucket

Fine-mesh net

NET RESULTS
Nets have different mesh
sizes, for large or small specimens.
Exercise caution, so as not to uproot plants.
After sorting, replace the net's contents in the water
as quickly as possible.

Did you know?

AMAZING FACTS

The oldest goldfish known about lived to the ripe old age of 43. On average, goldfish can survive for 20–30 years and a well-kept koi (from the carp family) can live for about 50 years.

Mayflies, found near rivers and ponds, are sometimes called "dayflies" because of their short lifespan. After spending up to three years underwater as nymphs, adult mayflies often die just a few hours after maturing and rarely live for more than a few days. This is because the adults do not have functioning mouths or digestive systems, and therefore cannot feed.

Newts sometimes migrate long distances to breed. They often travel back to the pond where they grew up, finding their way by sight and smell.

The largest dragonfly ever known is a fossilized specimen from the USA, with a wingspan of about 60 cm (24 in) – more than three times the size of today's record holder.

Historically, Native Americans in North America have found many uses for pond lilies. The roots were used medicinally, applied externally to wounds and eaten to cure digestive ailments. The roots, leaves, and buds of the plant were also used for food, and even the seeds were fried and eaten, or ground into flour.

Historically, pond lily has been used as food

Tympanum

Tree frog

Like mammals, frogs have ears on the sides of their heads, but the eardrum, or tympanum, is outside instead of inside the skull. A frog's call is very loud for the animal's size, which raises the question as to how a frog avoids blowing its own eardrums. It may be because a frog's ears are connected to its lungs, so that the vibrations created by its call are felt not just in the eardrums, but throughout the body.

There are around 400 species of frogs and 300 species of toads.

Duckweed

The cane toad (*Bufo marinus*) lays 35,000 eggs a year, more than any other amphibian.

The world's muddiest river is the Yellow River, China, which deposits silt over its flood plain and delta, covering an area of 141,645 sq km (54,690 sq miles). It is estimated that 2.04 billion tonnes (2 billion tons) of soil is deposited annually.

The smallest flowering plant in the world is *Wolffia angusta*, a species of duckweed that is found in Australia. With each plant measuring just 0.8 mm (0.031 in) long and 0.4 mm (0.015 in) wide, a tablespoon can hold up to 100,000. It's no surprise that duckweed also holds the record for the world's smallest fruit. Measuring about 0.25 mm (0.01 in) long, these fruits weigh just 70 micrograms (0.00002 oz), which is about 4 billion times lighter than the world's biggest fruit, the squash.

The Kenai river, Alaska, USA, was home to the world's largest salmon, which weighed 44 kg (97.4 lb).

River otters sometimes travel across land, usually in search of a mate. They move by running a few steps and then sliding on their bellies. One slide can be as long as 6 m (20 ft) and may reach a speed of 29 k/ph (18 mph).

Fishing bats have echolocation so sophisticated that they can detect a minnow fish's fin as fine as a human hair protruding only 2 mm (0.08 in) above a pond's surface.

The pond-dwelling water spider (*Argyroneta aquatica*) spends most of its life underwater by creating an air-filled "diving bell". It does this by weaving a waterproof home from silk thread and securing it to plants just below the water line. The spider then uses special hairs on its skin to trap bubbles of air at the surface, which it inserts into the diving bell until full. The home becomes inflated with trapped air and creates a sealed unit in which the spider can live and lay eggs. The spider must gather new air bubbles regularly to maintain fresh oxygen.

If algae, the microscopic plant organisms that live in ponds, overgrow, they can cause great harm by exhausting the available oxygen supplies. Without enough oxygen, a pond's plants and animals will soon die.

QUESTIONS AND ANSWERS

Q What's the difference between a pond and a lake?

A A pond is a body of water that is shallow enough to support rooted plants, is fairly even in temperature all over, and is usually covered in mud at the bottom because the water is generally still. A lake is bigger than a pond and is too deep to support rooted plants, except near the shore. Some lakes are big enough for waves to be produced and may vary significantly in temperature from top to bottom. A pond is small enough to freeze solid during very cold winter spells, whereas a lake may freeze over, but is unlikely to freeze solid.

Q Do frogs have teeth?

A Most frogs do have teeth of a sort. They have maxillary teeth, a ridge of very small teeth around the upper edge of the jaw, and vomerine teeth, tiny teeth on the roof of the mouth. However, because most frogs have no teeth on the lower jaw, they can only grip and not chew their food, which they have to swallow whole. Toads, on the other hand, have no teeth at all.

Q What is the largest freshwater fish?

A The giant Pirarucu (*Arapaima gigas*) is the largest freshwater fish in the world and is native to the Amazon and Orinoco rivers in South America. The largest specimens caught have been recorded as weighing 200 kg (440 lb). Also called the Amazon Redtail because of the bright crimson colour of its tail, this fish has very rough scales, which are used as sandpaper and nail files by local peoples. As a result of overfishing, this species is endangered, and international trade has been banned to help the stock to recover. As part of a conservation project, specimens have been transported to Thailand to breed in the Bung Sam Lan lake.

The Pirarucu fish is hunted for its meat

Q What is the fiercest freshwater predator?

A The piranha fish is probably the most ferocious freshwater animal you can find. Native to the Amazon river, these fish have very powerful jaws and razorsharp teeth and can strip a carcass in seconds. Piranhas have been known to attack animals as large as goats. There are many different types of piranha, however, and not all are carnivorous. Some are vegetarian and eat no meat at all. Even meat-eating piranhas eat only fruit and nuts for much of the year. Native Americans use the jaws of piranhas to create tools for cutting wood and hair.

Q Can pond snails breathe underwater?

A No, but they can hold their breath for sustained periods of time. A pond snail takes in air from the surface of the pond using a special hole in its body. Above the water line, this hole sucks in air to its lung, but underwater the hole seals up.

Q How can you tell if a pond or river is polluted?

Piranha

A Water quality is most accurately measured by scientific tests, which determine factors such as pH levels, clarity, and temperature. However, even without conducting any tests, the presence or absence of plant and animal life can act as indicators of pollution. If a habitat is unhealthy, insects are the first to disappear. Mayflies, stoneflies, and some types of beetle are particularly sensitive to pollution. Fish such as trout and minnow can only live in clean water, whereas goldfish and carp are more hardy and can survive some types of pollution. Most plants cannot grow in unclean waters.

Record Breakers

SMALLEST FISH
• The smallest living fish is the tiny Philippino dwarf pygmy goby (*Pandaka pygmaea*), which lives in fresh water and is just 8mm (0.31 in) in length.

MOST SHOCKING FISH
• The electric eel (*Electrophorus electricus*) that lives in the Amazon river in South America can stun or kill its prey with a single electric shock.

BIGGEST FROG
• The body of the African goliath frog (*Conraua goliath*) measures 30 cm (12 in) in length and its outstretched legs add another 40 cm (16 in).

LONGEST RIVER
• The Nile river in Africa is the longest in the world at 6,825 km (4,241 miles).

LARGEST RIVER SYSTEM
• The Amazon river in South America is by far the biggest river system in the world. Its drainage basin is almost 6.2 million sq km (2.4 million sq miles).

HIGHEST WATERFALL
• Angel Falls, on the Churún river in Venezuela, South America, drops 979 m (3,212 ft) from Devil's Mountain.

Around the world

POND AND RIVER environments around the world vary greatly from continent to continent and from climate to climate. Tiny ponds in Europe have very different plant and animal life to that found in the mighty Amazon river in South America or the frozen ponds of northern Canada. Here are some examples of the amazing flora and fauna that can be found in freshwater environments in different regions. Your local natural history museum is a great place to discover more examples for yourself.

AFRICAN FISH EAGLE
The predatory African fish eagle (*Haliaeetus vocifer*) is common in Africa, and is usually found near rivers and coasts. It feeds mainly on fish and amphibians, but in some areas also preys on flamingoes and other water birds.

WESTERN POND TURTLE
The Western pond turtle (*Clemmys marmorata*) is only found in the states of Washington, Oregon, and California in the USA. These creatures can live for up to 50 years. They are extremely shy and will quickly hide at the first sign of a human presence.

PINK FRESHWATER DOLPHIN
One of only five freshwater species of dolphin in the world, the pink dolphin (*Inia geoffrensis*) is found in the Amazon and Orinoco rivers in South America. It has a hump on its back instead of a fin and is a very intelligent animal. Humans are the only real predators of this species, and due to overfishing and destruction of its habitat, the survival of the pink dolphin is now endangered.

Dolphins have very sharp teeth

Western pond turtles like to bask in the sun during the warm months

THAI WATERFALL

This is one of the many waterfalls in Phu Kradung nature reserve in northern Thailand. This river runs down a mountain that rises 1,325 m (4,240 ft) above sea level, and the aquatic habitat high up the mountain is unusual in Thailand's tropical climate. The cool temperatures at the top of the mountain mean that many of the plants are those of a temperate climate, and include pine forests and maple trees.

Arctic lichen by a frozen pond in Canada

ARCTIC LICHEN

There are almost 1,000 types of Arctic lichen growing in North America. Lichens are a cross between fungi and algae and can survive for up to 5,000 years. They can withstand great extremes of temperature and grow on almost any surface, including rock, tree bark, bones, and animal dung. They are the chief winter food of moose and caribou.

This toad is an excellent swimmer, but can only crawl on land, not hop

AFRICAN CLAWED TOAD

The African clawed toad (*Xenopus laevis*) has existed for about 125 million years. Native to sub-Saharan Africa, these toads spend most of their lives in water and very little on land. During dry spells they can submerge themselves in mud without moving or eating for periods of up to a year, while they wait for rain to fall.

ETANG DE BERRE

The Etang de Berre (Berre pond) is part of the delta of the Rhône river in the South of France. In recent years this habitat has suffered severe pollution as a result of heavy industry in the area. This has had disastrous consequences for plants and animals that live in and around the water.

Find out more

THERE ARE MANY WAYS to find out more about pond and river life. If you live near a pond or river, you can study the changes a freshwater habitat undergoes through the seasons. Using a notebook and camera, record the different plant and animal life that you come across. A natural history museum will contain information about the history and evolution of species. A day out fishing or following a riverside trail will allow you to observe and enjoy the teeming life of an aquatic habitat. You can also breed your own fish and grow plants in an aquarium at home.

GO FISHING
Fishing is a very popular sport and pastime. A visit to an angling shop will provide you with the kit you need. Accompanied by an adult, find a calm spot on a river or large pond on public land and set up. Be patient – fishing requires quiet concentration. When you catch a fish, always release it back unharmed into the water.

STUDYING FROGSPAWN
One of the most fun ways to explore pond life is to chart the growth of frogspawn into adult frogs. Spring is the season to look for frogspawn, which is created when a male frog fertilizes eggs laid in the water by a female. The eggs are protected by jelly, which floats to the surface. After about two weeks the spawn will hatch into tadpoles, which continue to develop for five weeks before they reach adulthood.

Frogspawn

Spawn of common frog can contain up to 3,000 eggs

Pond surfaces are often overgrown with lilies

POND LIFE
Find out where your nearest pond is. You may know someone who has a pond in their back garden, or it might involve a trip to a local park or nature reserve. Both manmade and natural ponds are miniature worlds, alive with plants, fish, insects, and frogs. Use a notebook to record the species you find there.

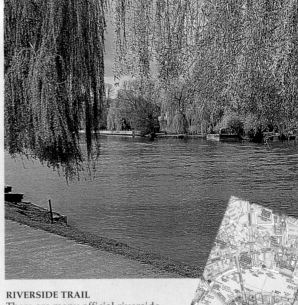

RIVERSIDE TRAIL
There are many official riverside walks. Your local conservation society will have more details. The trail shown here is the Thames path in England, which starts in the Cotswold hills and ends at the Thames Barrier in London.   Thames map

HOME AQUARIUM

Rearing fish as pets in a freshwater aquarium can be very rewarding. This tank is a cold water aquarium containing an array of goldfish, including the common goldfish, the comet, or single-tailed goldfish, and "fancy", or fantailed, goldfish. An aquarium also allows you to grow aquatic plants. Fish and plants must be well cared for on a daily basis.

USEFUL WEBSITES

- Froggyville: Adopt your own virtual pet frog!
  www.froggyville.com
- Tropica: An online plant store with a comprehensive illustrated database dedicated to aquatic plants.
  www.tropica.com
- Online aquarium for kids: An alternative to keeping a real aquarium – and lots of tips for the real world too!
  www.twilightbridge.com/hobbies/aquariums/index.htm
- The Aquatic Ecology Page: In-depth list of web resources.
  www.nysfola.org/alinks/

NATURAL HISTORY MUSEUM

Any natural history museum will house exhibits of both preserved and living plant and animal specimens from pond and river habitats. These students and their teachers are studying living fire-bellied toads and their tadpoles.

Places to visit

CAIRNGORM NATIONAL NATURE RESERVE, SCOTLAND, UK
Aquatic attractions at Britain's largest nature reserve include a working fish farm, where you can feed the trout, and fishing facilities.

AIGAS DAM FISH LIFT, AIGAS, SCOTLAND, UK
The dam has a specially constructed fish ladder to allow Scottish salmon to make their way upstream. A viewing facility allows visitors to watch the salmon pass through.

MARGAM RIVERBANK POND CENTRE, NEATH PORT TALBOT, WALES, UK
A fascinating exhibition that tells the story of a river from spring to sea and covers the flora and fauna of local freshwater environments.

NATURAL HISTORY MUSEUM, SOUTH KENSINGTON, LONDON, ENGLAND, UK
With exhibitions dedicated to fish, amphibians, plants, fossils, ecology, and birds, the life galleries hold plenty in store for eager students.

THAMES PATH NATIONAL TRAIL
Running from the source of the river in the Cotswolds to the Thames Barrier, London, this amazing riverside trail covers 288 km (179 miles). Part of the trail can be covered in one day or a family holiday could be organised around the walk.

ENVIRONMENTAL EDUCATION CENTRE, KELHAM ISLAND CENTRE, SHEFFIELD, UK
School education sessions covering pond and river life centred on the River Don, its weir, and a waterwheel built in 1210!

A school visit to the Natural History Museum, London, England

Glossary

ALGA Microscopic plants that grow in sunlit water containing phosphates, nitrates, and other nutrients. Algae, like all aquatic plants, add oxygen to the water and are important in the food chain.

AMPHIBIAN A class of cold-blooded vertebrates, typically gill-breathing in the larval state and lung-breathing or skin-breathing as adults.

ALLUVIUM Sediment or loose material comprised of clay, silt, sand, gravel, and larger rocks deposited by moving water.

APPENDAGE An attached feature to the body of an animal.

AQUATIC Organisms that live or grow in a water environment.

ARTHROPOD A member of a major division of the animal kingdom with segmented bodies and joined appendages, such as crustaceans and insects.

BACTERIA Microscopic organisms without chlorophyll that multiply by simple division, often feeding on dead organisms.

BARBEL A freshwater fish of the carp family with beard-like appendages at its mouth.

BIVALVE An animal with a shell in two parts or valves, such as an oyster.

Creeping jenny, a hardy plant

The estuary of a river, where its journey ends

BRACT A small leaf-like flap that grows just beneath a flower.

CANAL A constructed open channel for transporting water.

CARNIVORE An animal or plant that feeds on flesh.

CHLOROPHYLL The green pigment present in most plants and central to the process of photosynthesis.

CRUSTACEAN A member of a large class of arthropod animals with hard shells, such as crabs, lobsters, shrimps, and barnacles.

DORSAL FIN The fin at the back or rear of a fish's body.

ECOSYSTEM A community of organisms and their environment.

EROSION The wearing away of rock or soil by the gradual detachment of soil or rock fragments by water, wind, and ice.

ESTUARY The wide, lower tidal part of a river where it flows into the ocean.

FROND A leaf or leaf-like organism, especially relating to palms and ferns.

FRY Young fishes just hatched, or a young salmon in its second year of life.

GASTROPOD A class of assymetrical molluscs, including limpets, snails, and slugs, in which the foot is broad and flat and the shell, if any, is in one piece and conical.

Snail pond, a gastropod

GRAVEL A loose natural collection of rounded rock fragments on a river bed.

HABITAT The physical environment or normal abode of a plant or animal.

HARDY Relating to plants that can withstand extremes of temperature, including frost.

HERBIVORE An animal that eats only grass or other plants.

HERMAPHRODITE A plant or animal with the organs of both sexes.

INSECTIVORE An animal that feeds only on insects.

LARVA An animal in a developing or immature state that is markedly different from full adult development.

LATERAL LINE A line along the side of a fish's body that marks the position of a sensory organ.

MAMMAL A large class of warm-blooded vertebrates that suckle their young and generally have a covering of hair.

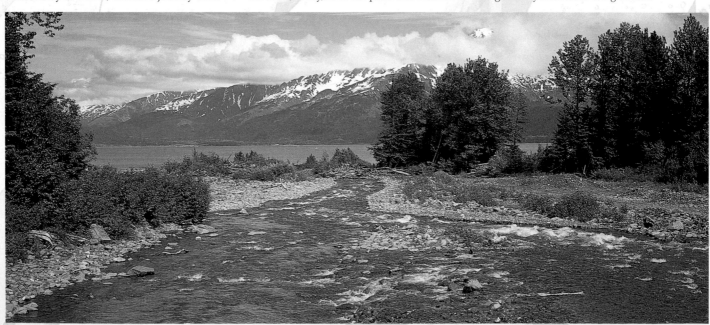

MARGINAL Plants that grow around the edge of water.

METAMORPHOSIS The series of changes that an insect undergoes between its early life and adulthood. Insects that undergo incomplete metamorphosis change gradually as they grow up. Ones that undergo complete metamorphosis change abruptly, during a resting stage called a pupa. In both cases, growth normally stops once the adult stage is reached.

MONOTREME A mammal that reproduces by laying eggs. Unlike other mammals, monotremes have a single opening for their reproductive and digestive systems.

NYMPH An immature form of some insects, such as the mayfly or the dragonfly, similar to the adult but with wings and underdeveloped sex organs.

ORGANISM A living thing.

OMNIVORE An organism that feeds on both animal and plant food.

OVERWINTER When plants or animals stay alive throughout the winter season.

PARR A young salmon of up to two years of age, before it becomes a smolt.

PECTORAL FIN The anterior, or front-facing, pair of fins on a fish.

PERENNIAL A plant that lasts or flowers for more than two years.

PULMONATE An organism that has lungs, or similar organs.

PETAL One of the brightly coloured leaf-like parts of a flower.

PHOTOSYNTHESIS The process by which plants generate their own food, created when a green pigment called chlorophyll reacts with sunlight, carbon dioxide, and water to make carbohydrates, water, and oxygen.

PHYTOPLANKTON The plant-like component of plankton, consisting mainly of microscopic algae.

PLANKTON Minute organisms, including animal and algae, that are found in the surface layers of water. Plankton drifts with the current.

Phytoplankton, visible only under a microscope

POLLINATION The process by which pollen is carried from one flower to another. The male pollen fertilizes the female ovule and creates a seed. Insects or animals often carry pollen between flowering plants, or it can be blown by the wind.

PUPATION A passive stage in the development of an insect from larva to adult.

RAPIDS Fast, swirling currents that form where river water flows down a steep slope.

RHIZOME A creeping underground stem. Rhizomes often sprout leaves as they push their way through the ground.

SEPAL A leafy flap that protects a flower while it is still a bud. Sepals often fall off when the flower opens.

SMOLT A young river salmon when it is bluish along the upper half of its body and silvery along the sides.

SOURCE The starting point of a river, usually from a natural water spring that emerges at high altitudes from beneath the Earth.

SPAWN A mass of eggs laid in water, such as those laid by frogs.

STYLE The slender part of a flower that connects the stigma, which receives the pollen, and the ovary, which produces eggs.

TRIBUTARY A stream that flows into another stream, river, or lake.

VERTEBRATE Any animal that has a backbone. This group includes mammals, fish, birds, reptiles, and amphibians.

VENTRAL FIN Either of the paired fins on the belly of a fish.

WATERFALL A vertical cascade of water where a river plunges over hard rock.

YEARLING A one-year old fish.

The source of a river is often very small

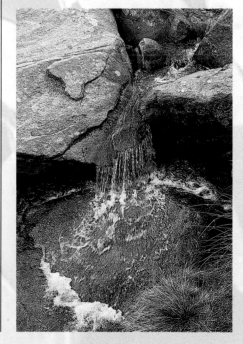

The trout only survives in freshwater habitats

Index

Acknowledgements

Dorling Kindersley would like to thank the following:

The Booth Museum of Natural History, Brighton.
Ed Wade and Respectable Reptiles, Hampton, for help with the amphibians and reptiles.
Richard Harrison and Robert Hughes, Upwey Trout Hatchery for help with the trout eggs.
Jane Parker for the index.
Fred Ford and Mike Pilley of Radius Graphics, and Ray Owen for artwork.
Anne-Marie Bulat for her work on the initial stages of the book.
Carole Ash, Neville Graham, and Marytn Foote for design assistance.
Kim Taylor for special photography on page 27.
Dave King for special photography on pages 2–5, 28–31, 36–37, 52–53, and 62–63.
David Burnie for consultancy.

The author would like to thank the following:

Don Bentley for loan of equipment; Mike Birch of Mickfield Fish Centre, Max Bond and Tim Watts of Framlingham Fisheries; CEL Trout Farm, Woodbridge; Keith Chell and Chris Riley of Slapton Ley Field Centre; Wendy and David Edwards, Ellen and Chris Nall, Jacqui and Tony Storer for allowing their ponds to be sampled; David Gooderham and Jane Parker for help with collecting; Andrea Hanks and staff at Thornham Magna Field Centre; Alastair MacEwan for technical advice; Ashley Morsely for fish care; Richard Weaving of Dawlish Warren Nature Reserve; John Wortley, Andy Wood and Anglian Water Authority.

Picture credits

t = top; b = bottom; m = middle; l = left; r = right

Heather Angel: 43 tr; 45 br; 53 br
G I Bernard/Oxford Scientific Films: 51ml
B Borrell/Frank Lane Picture Agency: 39m
David Boyle/Animals Animals/Oxford Scientific Films: 66b
Bridgeman Art Library: 34tr
British Museum/Natural History: 48tl
Jane Burton/Bruce Coleman Ltd: 64bl
B B Casals/Frank Lane Picture Agency: 39t
John Clegg: 47tl
G Dore/Bruce Coleman Ltd: 48mr; 60tr
Fotomas Index: 39ml
EPA/Press Association Picture Library: 67bl
Mary Evans Picture Library: 22tl; 23tr; 30bl; 40tr
C B and D W Frith/Bruce Coleman Ltd: 41br
Tom and Pam Gardener/Frank Lane Picture Agency: 38br
D T Grewcock/Frank Lane Picture Agency: 62br; 71br
Mark Hamblin/Frank Lane Picture Agency: 39bm
David Hosking/Eric and David Hosking: 27m; 37ml
E & D Hosking/FLPA – Images of Nature: 67c, 70b
Zig Leszczynski/Oxford Scientific Films: 65bl
Mansell Collection: 13m, tr, ml; 35ml; 49br
L C Marigo/Bruce Coleman Ltd: 42bl
W Meinderts/Foto Natura/FLPA – Images of Nature: 65tr
The Natural History Museum, London: 69b
Oxford Scientific Films: 71t
Fritz Polking/FLPA – Images of Nature: 67tl
Dr Morely Reed/Science Photo Library: 39bl
Jany Sauvanet/Natural History Photographic Agency: 40ml
Richard Vaughan/Ardea: 58mr
Alan Weaving/Ardea: 66tl
Roger Wilmshurst/Frank Lane Picture Agency: 29t
Norbert Wu/Still Pictures: 66c

Illustrations by Coral Mula:
34bl; 36ml, bl, br; 35tl, ml; 38ml, m; 39mt

Picture research by:
Millie Trowbridge